"Perhaps the richest contribution of Richard Hart's *Preaching: The Secret to Parish Revival* is the abundance of references he offers from the many contemporary writers in the field of homiletics. So well acquainted is Father Hart with the literature, that his work weaves an overview of the dynamics of effective liturgical preaching from virtually all of the current wisdom available. With a style that is simple and conversational, he offers brief but salient chapters on the many dimensions that are necessary for the revival of parish preaching."

Rev. Joseph J. Juknialis
Director of the Preaching Institute,
Saint Francis Seminary

"Having taught homiletics for twenty years I can honestly claim that Father Hart's book, *Preaching: The Secret to Parish Revival* is invaluable for novice and advanced preachers alike. The chapters on Creativity, Simple Language, and Good Imagery are not only insightful but also illustrate the author's own creative use of imagery and simple language throughout his book. It ought to be a 'must' on every preacher's reading list."

Rev. Andre Papineau, S.D.S.
Author, *Sermons for Sermon Haters*
Associate Professor of Pastoral Studies,
Sacred Heart School of Theology
Hales Corners, WI

"Richard Hart's book will be welcomed by those looking for practical suggestions for preaching that are written in an easy-to-read style. Nothing fancy; just down to earth ideas and comments on preaching. Someone preparing to preach for the first time or one who has preached for years will equally appreciate this resource."

Jim Alt
Editor/Publisher
Deacon Digest Magazine

Preaching
The Secret to Parish Revival

RICHARD HART, O.F.M.Cap.

TWENTY-THIRD PUBLICATIONS
BAYARD Mystic, CT 06355

Dedication

To my mother, Sylvia.

Twenty-Third Publications/Bayard
185 Willow Street
P.O. Box 180
Mystic, CT 06355
(860) 536-2611
(800) 321-0411

ISBN:1-58595-021-1
Library of Congress Catalog Card Number: 00-131183
Printed in the U.S.A.

Contents

INTRODUCTION

Recently, Andrew Greeley wrote an article entitled "A Catholic Revival?" which appeared in the April 10, 1999 issue of *America*. In this article, Greeley writes:

> I would suggest that the secret of revival in the last century was good preaching and that the secret of a revival today might also be good preaching. This preaching would have to be parish-centered because parishes are where most people are. The preaching would have to focus on the core beliefs of Christianity. It would have to be excellent (less than one out of five American Catholics think that the homilies they hear are excellent). Such a suggestion might seem utopian. It probably is, given the reluctance of many Catholic clerics to do anything to improve the quality of their preaching or, for that matter, the quality of the Sunday liturgy.

If only one out of five American Catholics think the homilies they hear in church are excellent, then we are surely in need of a revival in parish preaching. This book was written in the hope that the suggestions offered here would help all preachers enact such a revival in their own parishes. The reader will find practical advice on how to improve homily content, especially in areas that are not treated extensively in other books. Also highlighted are several key elements that help make a good homily: relevance, creativity, good imagery, stories, appropriate humor, passion, and simplicity in language.

Oftentimes, preachers are not willing to acknowledge that homily preparation is hard work and demands much discipline. This can create a feeling that preaching is a chore rather than a joy, and lead to a minimum of preparation time. Yet even the preacher with little natural skill can put together a good homily with the right amount of preparation.

Good preaching is preeminently a prayer event, and good preachers share their prayer life with listeners. The more they immerse themselves into praying with Scripture, the less time they will spend retelling the scriptural text in their homily, instead offering effective insights. The more they have prepared and prayed over Scripture, the more they will be able to preach God's Word with passion and enthusiasm. Good preachers believe in the efficacy of God's word and preach with fire in their bellies.

A good homily not only informs and delights but persuades. A preacher has to be a prophet challenging listeners as the prophets did, especially the greatest prophet, Jesus. Prophetic preaching challenges listeners to new ways of thinking, to change our mindsets, so we can look at things differently.

Above all, our homilies have to be based on Scripture. This does not mean we give lip service to a few scriptural passages. Rather, it means that our preaching is shaped by Scripture. The biblical message must be the starting point and foundation of our preaching.

It has been said that the gospel well proclaimed is the homily half proclaimed. As preachers, we proclaim God's inspired word then offer an interpretation and application to the lives of all in the assembly.

Homilies can change the lives of those who hear them. With time, effort, and the fire of enthusiasm, you can become a preacher who influences the lives of others with the gospel message. Are you ready for a revival in *your* preaching?

Note: This book cites passages from the liturgical document *Fulfilled in Your Hearing: The Homily in the Sunday Assembly*, published by the United States Catholic Conference in 1982. This excellent document is an invaluable resource for any preacher.

1   IS IT RELEVANT?

Just as there are a variety of ways to present homilies, so there are a similar number of ways to prepare a homily. The first step is to analyze one's audience or assembly. This approach is often overlooked or taken for granted.

The document *Fulfilled in Your Hearing: The Homily in the Sunday Assembly,* written by the Bishops' Committee on Priestly Life and Ministry in 1982, states: "We believe that it is appropriate, indeed essential, to begin this treatment of the Sunday homily with the assembly rather than with the preacher or the homily..." (#4). The document goes on to give two main reasons for this statement. The first is that communication theorists emphasize the importance of having a good understanding of one's audience. The second reason is based on contemporary ecclesiology: when we come together for liturgy we are a church gathered in the Lord where we continue to renew our covenant with God.

And so a good homily always keeps the audience in mind and addresses real life issues in light of a Scripture perspective. When a preacher fails to analyze the audience, the homily will most likely lack relevance to the listeners. Preachers can offer many exegetical insights concerning the reading, but without relevance the response may well be "So what?" or "Big deal!"

God's Word, found in Scripture, should help people relate to the human events happening in their lives. Preachers need to take the mystery of faith found in the Scripture readings and show how this same mystery is happening in the lives of people today. The task is to make Scripture come alive and help people see Jesus. When this happens it is a *cor ad cor* experience, a heart interacting with the hearts of other faith-filled people.

Preachers should be aware that one of the first things hearers often do is excuse themselves from the homily: "I'm not a prostitute, a prodigal son or daughter, or a tax collector who cheats, so this does not apply to me." And so the challenge is to make each listener feel that in some way, they are included in the homily—no matter what their station in life. One preacher did this by inviting everyone (including himself) who was perfect to come forward. No one did; in this way, he involved each listener in what he had to say. He then went on to show how each of us is imperfect and in need of conversion.

Preachers can involve their listeners by tapping into a universal experience such as pain or suffering. Another technique is to name a demon like greed, racism, or idolatry, and offer some concrete suggestions on how to claim and tame it. A sure-fire way to turn *off* listeners is for preachers to address topics that are relevant to themselves but not to the assembly, or that apply to a limited group of hearers. An even greater temptation is to preach on one's favorite topics and avoid subjects with which we are not very comfortable. The criticism of the English essayist Thomas Carlyle might apply here: "If that man had anything to say, he could say it."

Making connections

As mentioned before, preachers need to make connections between Scripture and the daily lives of those in the assembly. In this regard, Jesus is an ideal model for preachers because he talked about things that people could readily understand and identify with: the lilies of the field, vines and branches, sheep and shepherds, seeds and sowing, weeds and wheat, just to mention a few. Jesus illustrated his words by using parables, stories that were easy for people to relate to because they concerned practical and earthy matters.

The challenge is to preach about something that continues to happen today, not something that happened 2,000 years ago. Jesus proclaimed the good news in the synagogue by first quoting a passage from Isaiah: "The Spirit of the Lord is upon me…". He then spoke to the here and now by saying, "Today this scripture has been fulfilled in your hearing" (Lk 4:18, 21).

4

Some homilists presume that they can escort people to the Holy Land or other spots in biblical antiquity with the ease of a magic wand. Some preachers try to dramatize events in the lives of John the Baptist, Jesus, Mary, and Joseph or other persons of Scripture. Yet it is difficult to thoroughly explain most of these events within the usual timeframe allowed for a homily. To make Scripture relevant, preachers have to present it in the here and now.

When the homily comforts or confronts the hearer in present terms, it is not the homilist but the Word of God that has an impact. As Peter writes in his epistle, "Whoever speaks must do so as one speaking the very words of God..." (1 Pt 4:11). Each preacher adds one's own nuance or a new dimension to the homily by addressing the real needs of real people. In this way preachers become windows that let light into the lives of people in the assembly.

The pain, struggles, doubts, concerns, sorrows, and joys of every member of the assembly can be seen in relation to Scripture. This does not mean preachers have to answer every question or solve every problem with a homily. Our words will not stop violence, lower unemployment, or bring back a teenager killed in a tragic accident. Yet preachers can use Scripture to point out that all life is a mystery to be lived—not solved. We can show how Jesus identified with our pain, struggles, doubts, concerns, sorrows, and joys, and how he responded to these emotions. As Jesus showed the apostles the wounds in his hands and his side, so must each preacher, in ways subtle or not, share their very real experience with the congregation.

An effective preacher needs to be sensitive, involved in and exposed to all reality, and then endeavor to apply the balm of Gilead to people's wounds. To expound on sophisticated theories or deep theological questions when people need to be inspired, hope-filled, and motivated to live better lives is like quarrying stone with a razor blade. The words of Jeremiah can well be a warning to each of us: "All they ever offer to my deeply wounded people are empty hopes for peace" (6:14).

An awareness of the assembly's needs
Our preaching is greatly enhanced by knowing parishioners' lives, by

recognizing your audience. Pastors and pastoral associates have a distinct advantage in this regard because they often know their parishioners well. They can look out at the assembly and see Marie, whose husband recently died at the age of forty-five; Joe, who has been unemployed for over six months; Colleen, who just got a divorce after a bitter custody battle; and sixteen-year-old Becky, who seriously contemplated suicide. One pastor with whom I am acquainted knows his eleven hundred parishioners so well that he is able to call them all by their first names.

How can we stay in contact with our parishioners? A few of the ways to keep in touch are by our involvement in parish organizations, with counseling sessions, by visiting the sick at home and in the hospital, by offering the sacrament of reconciliation, with social visits, or just by being with people as a friend.

Preachers can find out what people are thinking and feeling, as well their everyday concerns, by actively listening. This must become a way of life for us. Preachers should be careful not to engage in a monologue where they end up listening to their own voices. Active listening means becoming more attuned to what others are saying. This is critical, because just one word can sometimes be misunderstood. Here's a good illustration: a certain dentist was asking for more light from his assistant so he could see better. The elderly man in the chair understood him to say "bite," so he bit the dentist's hand.

Often we just don't listen to what others are saying to us. I know of a groom who, at his wedding, wanted to find out if people were really listening to him. While standing in the reception line, he said to the people as he shook hands with them, "My grandmother died last night." Few, if any, heard what he said—or at least reacted. His bride heard him, however, and kicked him in the shins. But this proved to be a powerful experiment for the couple. Now, whenever one of them feels the other is not listening, he or she says, "My grandmother died."

Psychologist Carl R. Rogers defines good listening as having unconditional positive regard for the other person. Jesus exemplified just this in his relationships with other people. No wonder his Father was so well pleased with him and said: "This is my Son, my Chosen; listen to him!" (Lk 9:35).

The sensitive preacher takes into account the concerns, attitudes and viewpoints of the hearers. Good preachers help hearers to recognize their own concerns, and realize God's love and concern for them. Do you know what the attitudes of your parishioners are toward poverty, violence, welfare, and social justice? What are their values and goals? One preacher claimed that a person who did not have doubts against faith could not be a true Christian. Upon hearing this, an elderly nun in the audience burst into tears. We must be sensitive to the needs of our assembly.

The essence of understanding others is often expressed in this ancient proverb: "You cannot understand your brother (or sister) unless you have walked in his (her) moccasins for many miles." Martin Buber expressed it more succinctly: "Experience the other side." Good preachers know their listeners and are attuned to their concerns. They make an effort to get on the same wavelength.

Who are they?

Senior citizens, baby boomers, generation X-ers, and teenagers each have different outlooks on life. What are these outlooks, and how does a preacher address them effectively, especially when the assembly ranges in age from eight to eighty? Thieliche, who was one of Germany's great preachers, stated: "Sometime during each sermon I think I'm each kind of person. By the end of the sermon I hope to say something relevant for each kind, something which grips the person."

Another consideration is the religious education of the group on the whole. Words like "incarnational," "salvific," and "ecclesial" will fall on deaf ears unless the hearers have some kind of theological education. As one pastor observed: "Our church has people with scientific backgrounds who need to be spoken to scientifically. Their thoughts about God tend to focus on the concept of energy rather than on a personal God."

How often do you see members of the assembly in church? Are they daily worshipers? Weekend worshipers, or Christmas and Easter people? Those who worship on a daily or frequent basis usually hunger for deeper insights into God's Word. Some weekend worshipers also have a hunger, but many are apathetic. The people who come only once or twice a year present a real challenge because their needs are greater, especially in the area of conversion. Their faith is often as fragile as a spring flower.

As you can see, it is important to analyze one's audience or assembly very carefully so as to make our homilies more relevant. A relevant homily shares the moral dilemmas, anguish, pain, and search for meaning faced by many people today. It gives hearers something to think about and take home because it holds a mirror before them.

A relevant homily involves those who hear it. Above all, a relevant homily leaves the assembled with a clearer picture of Jesus, the primary model for Christian living.

2   Homiletic Pitfalls

J. Philip Wogaman writes: "To occupy the pulpit is a great privilege. It is a privilege that can be abused, either by failing to take our responsibility seriously enough or by using it manipulatively."

Let's look at some types of homilies that are not focused, and wander from subject to subject. In his writing, Thomas Aquinas used a technique where he would say what a certain topic was not before describing what it was. A similar process will be used here, but with more emphasis placed on the elements that make up a good homily.

Jericho preaching

Have you ever listened to a preacher walk around and around a topic, and never get to the heart of the message? The homily starts to feel like a merry-go-round, whose riders (the listeners) are silently screaming, "Stop! I want to get off." Usually because of poor preparation, some preachers extemporize, hoping to find a message in the process. This reminds me of a Family Circus cartoon I saw recently, which depicts a preacher mounting the pulpit while a little girl in the pew whispers to her brother, "This is the part he gets to make up by himself."

Good preaching is like an arrow hitting a bull's eye; its powerful message goes directly to the listeners. A preacher cannot hit the target by beating around the bush. The goal of an effective homily is to inspire comments like these: "Your homily made me feel like you knew me and my concerns. It seemed as though you were speaking directly to me," or "That preacher knows what is going on in my life."

To achieve directness, preachers need to identify and struggle with one single point that they want to convey. As Fr. Stephen Doyle states, "A simple homily that people will remember should make only one point....people turn off long, complex homilies." Try to crystalize your point in a single brief sentence. Imagine that you are sending a telegram and are charged for each word. Economize on the statement. Use one-syllable words rather than two- or three-syllable words. (A good example of the power and strength that can be conveyed with one-syllable words is found in the prologue of John's gospel.)

Your single point might be to instill in your listeners a spirit of gratitude, or to realize more deeply their selfishness, or to feel God's love for them, or to understand and name their real goal in life. If you want to find out whether you succeeded in getting your point across, ask someone who has heard the homily to sum it up in one sentence. Their answer might be most revealing.

The rocking chair

Most of us know the comfortable feeling of sitting in a rocking chair, going back and forth, back and forth, never getting anywhere. It's a wonderful way to relax. But rocking chair movement is not so wonderful in a homily. Listeners are left wondering: where are we going with this? The message of this kind of homily is often stale and colorless. Theological jargon is sometimes used, like "Holy Mother Church" or "Our Divine Lord." Bland platitudes are made in rapid succession and abstractions abound, both of which insure a dull homily. The homily has little, if any, nutritional value.

Good preaching is direct and gets right to the point. And so you must know exactly what your main idea or theme is; you must know exactly what needs to be proclaimed. Like a market analyst, the preacher looks for and determines the common denominator of the listeners in the pews.

When a preacher has presented the theme and stirred the interest of the assembly, one can then offer images and examples to develop the main point. For example, if the main point is exploring our innate fears, the preacher can state some of these fears: the loss of a loved one, contracting cancer, speaking in public, or not having enough money to pay the bills. Preachers can then show how important it is to deepen one's faith in light of our fears, remembering what Jesus said: "Take heart, it is I; do not be afraid" (Mt 14:27). Note that the expression "fear not" is repeated three hundred and sixty-five times in the Bible, once for every day of the year.

The wedding cake

Are your homilies like a wedding cake, all froth and icing but no real substance? Do they contain a lot of pious jargon and an overuse of sentimental thoughts? This kind of homily will not be crisis oriented, or share dilemmas, anguish, and pain. It will not search for meaning or address issues that make listeners cry or be inspired. It does not speak to the problems and needs of the assembly.

On the other hand, a forceful homily can address an issue of prejudice and convey one main point. You might begin by saying that Jesus often pointed out how the Jews were very prejudiced. During Jesus' time, if a Jew accidentally bumped into a Gentile, he would consider himself ritually unclean. Bringing this into modern times, a preacher might ask the listeners: if we are not prejudicial, why do many of us feel uncomfortable talking to a black person, an Oriental, or a native American? Why do we prefer one priest's style of liturgy to another's? Why won't we receive communion from a layperson? (Prejudice, by the way, has been described as "being down on something you are not up on.")

Paraphrasing the text

Do you try to get away with retelling the scriptural texts when you give a homily? It is far more effective to offer some insights of your own about the main idea. Merely repeating the scriptural texts often indicates a lack of preparation. This type of preaching is like a broken cistern that does not hold spiritual water.

Let's look at an example of insightful preaching using the parable of Dives, also known as "the rich man," and Lazarus (Lk 16:19–31). An obvious focus here would be on the gap between the rich and the poor. The parable might remind us of Charles Dickens's *Christmas*

Carol, and we can use this story to emphasize our point. (Dickens admitted that this parable inspired his famous book.) Pope John Paul II applied this parable to the rich and poor nations.

Another point to focus on in this parable might be the difference between being hungry and being full. Dives dines at a sumptuous banquet while Lazarus lies begging at the gate, his sores licked by dogs. You can contrast this with an example from Luke's gospel, where in the Sermon on the Plain, Jesus says, "Blessed are you who are hungry, for you will be satisfied. But woe to you who are filled now, for you will be hungry" (6:21,25).

The ho-hum homily

A preacher who does not capture the attention of the listeners in the first minute probably will not do so later. If preachers use an introduction like, "In today's gospel we hear…" they will surely receive a "ho-hum" response. Our first words have to break through the "ho-hum" mindset of our listeners, whose thoughts are often elsewhere: "Who's going to win the Packer game?" "What will I prepare for dinner?" "How am I going to lick a wicked golf slice?"

Begin your homily by using different kinds of introductions. One technique is to ask a provocative question, such as, "What is your greatest fear?" You can also open with a startling statement, like "Did you know that one out of four women has been sexually abused at some point in her life?" Statements like these can get listeners to pay attention. A brief story which echoes a point that will be pursued in the homily is appealing to most listeners. (But beware: a long, complicated, elaborate story often bewilders and confuses listeners!)

Have you heard the story about the little child who told the preacher that she was going to give him some money? The preacher asked why she was doing this. She replied, "Because my Daddy said you are one of the poorest preachers."

The head trip

Aim your preaching at the heart, and not the head. Don't make preaching a teaching event. A congregation or assembly comes to be engaged in the preaching event—not to be preached at. Moralistic preaching can often be characterized in this way because it is exhortative; according to Reinhold Niebuhr, it is the thinnest kind of preaching. "To the extent that we begin by moralizing about something, we cannot discover its true morality," Richard McCormick maintains. The goal of preaching should not be coercion but conversion.

"Head trip" preaching often utilizes theoretical, philosophical, and heavy theological language. Words like "eschatological," "metaphysical," "omniscience," and "salvific event" are tossed about like logs on a fire. Yet high-sounding language usually acts more like a blockade between the preacher and the listener, rather that the fuel that lights up the homily.

I recently came across this sentence: "Identity formation arises from the selective rejection and mutual assimilation of earlier identifications and their absorption into a new configuration." Huh? Not much is absorbed from impersonal erudition. Homilies are not meant to gloss over or shortchange the imperfections of listeners with glowing erudition, but to challenge them to deeper faith. Jesus did this by using vivid imagery to get his point across: the lilies in the field, the birds of the air, soil, seeds, rocks, and water.

Standing on a soapbox

This kind of homily centers on the preacher's favorite theme or pet peeve. These preachers often give the impression that they have the last word on a given subject. I've heard them described as "preachers in their pulpits...who speak ten feet above contradiction." Good preachers do not use the pulpit as a sounding board for their own pet peeves and problems. We are challenged to be like Jesus, and not offer pat answers to every problem or question.

Andre Papineau, SDS, puts it well: "When preachers give the impression that they are never confused, never lost, and have all the answers, beware! Preachers who glibly speak about God...do a disservice to the congregation's intelligence. On the other hand, when preachers acknowledge their uncertainties regarding God's will and express their confusion over perplexing issues, take heart! It is liberating to know that the preacher shares common ground with the congregation and isn't pontificating as if he or she had replaced Jesus at the right hand of the Father."

The primary goal of preaching should not be to give answers but to open listeners to what life really is all about, that is, a mystery to be lived and not solved. Good preaching helps listeners to think and choose. A meaningful message presents enough of a challenge. We should remember that "the Holy Spirit runs ahead of the preacher," as Karl Rahner wrote.

Whose words are they?

Most listeners will be able to tell whether or not you wrote your own homily. This brings us to homily services: these can benefit a preacher, but not if the homilies are repeated word for word. Too often, preachers do not make the message their own—which explains why the delivery lacks enthusiasm for the message or drones on in a monotone. It is difficult to get excited about someone else's ideas; they have to become our own.

Preachers need to speak from their own human experiences. Listeners are moved by what excites preachers and the Lord's action in their lives. John Henry Cardinal Newman expressed it well: "Heart speaks to heart." A good homily can be described as a faith-filled human heart speaking tenderly to other faith-filled hearts.

The lettuce homily

Many homilies conclude with "let us, then…(do this or that)." I call these "lettuce" homilies. The overuse of "let us…" can become trite and exhortatory. And most often, it is a waste of time to say it. People change their behavior because of need and experience, not because they are told to do so. A direct charge is far more effective in motivating listeners to act. Note that at the end of the parable about the Good Samaritan, Jesus simply said, "Go and do likewise," not "Let us do likewise." He also said, at the Last Supper, "Do this in memory of me," not "Let us do this in memory of me."

The conclusion to a homily, like the introduction, should be challenging and inspirational, and help listeners to encounter God. The ending is a good opportunity to stress or reemphasize the main point or central idea of the homily. For example, we might end a homily about courage by asking listeners to consider this: "Deep inside each one of us is a hero or a coward. Which one are you?" Or: "It takes more courage to face our darkness than our light. What do you choose to face?"

These are some examples of the types of homilies often heard within liturgy. Liturgical preaching is different from other forms of preaching, such as evangelizing, catechetical, or didactic preaching. Liturgical preaching should contribute to the liturgy, and is considered itself liturgy. It takes the liturgical event as its starting point. Again, it should emphasize the importance of a particular theme or point.

Within the context of the liturgy, the prayers, hymns, gestures, rites, seasons, feasts, eucharistic prayers—and, of course, the homily—all contribute to making Jesus' death and resurrection come alive for the assembly.

3 HOMILY PREPARATION IS NON-NEGOTIABLE

Eugene Burke, a Paulist preacher, once told a group of seminarians: "Going to bed with a woman is not the greatest sin a priest can commit. The greatest sin a priest can commit is to get up in the pulpit on a Sunday unprepared to preach." Some of us might not agree with that statement, but the point is well taken.

Most of us will agree that preparing a homily is hard work and demands much discipline. In his book, *Ten Responsible Minutes,* Joseph Manton, CSSR, offers three suggestions to becoming a good preacher: work, work, work. There are no shortcuts. Yet the good news is that people respond to well prepared homilies.

In preparing a homily, the preacher is sometimes led out into the desert where wild beasts roam and where there is no refreshing water to drink. Often, one's thoughts and words become entangled in a web of confusion and doubt. And so the temptation is to trivialize, extemporize, or "wing it." Another temptation is to retire from the struggle and give up, sitting under our broom tree like Elijah, sighing: "Is this preparation worth it all?"

A third temptation, which is all too familiar to us, is to turn on the television set and sit mesmerized for long periods of time. Or we might indulge in another form of gratification. If we feel hungry, we eat; if we feel lazy, we procrastinate. We might make a drink or smoke a cigarette, even being well aware of the consequences of these actions. Since we live in a society that offers instant coffee, easy credit, e-mail, and a host of other immediate gratifications, is it any wonder we long to reach for canned homilies and skip the slow process of proper preparation?

One way a preacher can be more effective is to collaborate with others in preparing the homilies. Some preachers have support groups to help in their preparation. *Fulfilled in Your Hearing* states it well: "an effective way for preachers to be sure that they are addressing some of the real concerns of the congregation in the homily is to involve members of that congregation in a homily preparation group. This can be done in a parish setting" (#106). (I have found this technique to be most valuable in my own homily preparation. It gives me different insights into the Scriptures, as well as ideas on how various people relate the texts to their daily lives.)

But most preachers prepare alone, and the work can be lonely, indeed. Paul alluded to this when he wrote to Timothy: "But the Lord stood by me and gave me strength, so that through me the message might be fully proclaimed and all the Gentiles might hear it" (2 Tim 4:17).

Chore or joy?

"Preaching makes me healthy. As soon as I open my mouth, all tiredness is gone." So spoke John Chrysostom concerning his well-known gift for dynamic preaching. How many of us are able to utter those words, or echo what Paul wrote to the Romans (1:15): "I am eager to preach the gospel"?

If preaching is a joy, it will motivate us to spend time preparing no matter what the cost. Those who find preaching a chore often end up with what might be called a microwave homily–rather than a crockpot homily. Crockpot cooking takes a long time. The food simmers and absorbs flavoring; the end of the process is usually a delicious meal. This is not always true of microwave cooking, which relies on speed. Good chefs make cooking look easy and enjoy what they do. Good preachers make preaching look easy and find joy in the work involved. This is what Dietrich Bonhoeffer referred to as "costly discipleship."

Most preachers use between seven and ten minutes to preach on a weekend, so every minute is vital to the homily. Walter Burghardt, SJ, maintains that he spends an hour for every minute he preaches.

No wonder he has been acclaimed as one of the outstanding preachers in the United States. He wrote at length how preaching "costs me my mind, costs me my spirit, costs me my flesh and blood."

It is also said that Archbishop Fulton Sheen spent a great deal of time preparing his television talks. Hours spent in preparation for a homily might seem excessive to many of us. Consider, however, the number of hours some of us spend counseling people. In that case, we reach only a few in comparison to the number of people we can reach on any given weekend.

I recently asked a priest, "When do you start preparing your homily?" He replied, "On Saturday." I don't think this is unusual. Some preachers wait until Friday or Saturday to put together a few frantic thoughts, then absolve themselves by saying they were too busy with other pastoral obligations. (Even worse are preachers who aren't busy and still find excuses!)

The ideal time to start preparing is on the Monday before you are to preach. For just as grapes need time to ferment and dough requires time to rise, so also good preaching takes time to be effective. *Fulfilled in Your Hearing* has the following advice: "A week of daily meditation on the readings of the following Sunday is not too much time to spend in preparation for the preaching we are called to do on the Lord's Day. Such regular preparation will allow us not only to savor the word in prayer but also to incorporate the experience of a full week into our preparation" (#21).

Authors of homiletic books often make distinctions between remote, intermediate, and immediate preparation. The goal of the remote stage is to gather sufficient ideas, insights, and images. This is also referred to as brainstorming. In the intermediate stage, we decide what material will be used. Here it is important to emphasize just one point that the preacher wants to convey. The goal of the immediate stage is to craft the homily into a well prepared work of art. This is the time to tighten the loose ends and make the proper connections.

Edward Braxton wrote in *A New Look at Preaching:* "The remote preparation of prayer and personal spirituality through which the preacher seeks ever to be open to conversion is essential if the preacher's words are to speak the hard and challenging truth of the gospel."

Preparation is hidden work, often a time of agony and desolation. We might recall the many years Jesus spent in quiet preparation before beginning his public life at age thirty. Look at a TV commercial, and how much is packed into minute or less. Long hours go into preparing these commercials. Proper preparation will convey that we consider the homily to be sacred time. It will better enable us to share with others the Word that has set us on fire.

Discipline

No matter how gifted or skilled the preacher, homily preparation demands a certain amount of discipline. Good preaching has been described as an incarnation, a time when words become flesh. But before that can happen, a preacher must be subjected to the crucible of discipline. (Did you know that the word "discipline" has its roots in the word "disciple"?)

The dictionary defines discipline as "a training that corrects, molds, or perfects the mental faculties or moral character; it is an orderly or prescribed conduct or pattern of behavior." Discipline helps us change, convert, or transform our vision or perception.

Discipline can be viewed as delayed satisfaction; this sense of the word is evident in the sports arena. Baseball, football, basketball, swimming, and other sports demand much practice and grueling exercise. Most football players will admit that they despise the training camps that help get them in shape for the season. Olympic competitors spend as much as seven hours a day practicing for an event, some of which last for only a few minutes. The satisfaction of winning a gold medal, the World Series, the Stanley Cup, or the Super Bowl does not diminish the exhausting hours of preparation.

The same kind of discipline is needed in other areas, such as music. Anyone who wishes to become proficient on an instrument will have to spend hours each day practicing. Archbishop Rembert Weakland, OSB, himself a gifted musician, states: "When I was a student at Juilliard, I noticed how many truly gifted students there were, some with a native ability that was outstanding. But soon I learned that not all of them would make it to the top, because so many did not have the discipline needed to perform consistently well and thus would dissipate their talents and time." These words can easily apply to preachers.

There is no substitute for discipline. The Book of Wisdom makes very clear what is needed to gain discipline: "For the first step toward discipline is a very earnest desire for her; then, care for discipline is love of her…" (6:17). No endeavor in life can succeed without some form of discipline. Do we really desire discipline and see how it will help us in becoming better preachers?

Anthony de Mello wrote: "When there's something within you that moves in the right direction, it creates its own discipline." As preachers, our motivation should be to share the good news, the word of God, with others.

Jesus was committed in his resolve to suffer, die, and rise for us. Preachers often have to ask themselves how committed they are to preaching "whether it is convenient or inconvenient," as Paul was. Paul knew "the time is coming when people will not put up with sound doctrine…and will turn away from listening to the truth….As for you, always be sober, endure suffering, do the work of an evangelist, carry out your ministry fully" (2 Tim 4:2–5).

Study

If we are to prepare our homilies well, serious study and reading, especially of Scripture, are absolutely necessary. The late Scripture scholar Raymond Brown gives a reason for immersing ourselves in Scripture: "All other works, patristic, Thomistic, and ecclesiastic, are words about God; only the Bible is the word of God." Jerome wrote that by constant reading and daily meditation he had made his breast a library of Christ.

Study means more than preparing for next week's homily. It means that we are well informed about a subject. Through regular study a preacher's faith life and character are formed; one's desk might even be said to become an altar. Study requires selecting the best and most qualified books, plenty of hard work, and setting aside a specific time and place to work with a minimum of interruptions. We might remember that small units of time spent here and there can prove just as valuable as lengthy periods.

Besides delving into Scripture, preachers should read other books: history, theology, biography, philosophy, and fiction, to name a few. Reaching back to the mystics or the early Church Fathers can pay rich dividends, and offer a new perspective on the interaction or attitudes of the characters in Scripture. We can glean important information about the news of the day from magazines, journals, and newspapers. These offer grist for our preaching.

If we come to the scriptural texts to plunder, C.S. Lewis once wrote, we are mistaken. We study a text which hopefully leads to prayer. We pray a text which leads to study. We come to learn the truth not just to produce a homily. Is the story coming true with us and in us, or without us?

A word is in order here about homily services: these can be a help or a hindrance to our preparation. The hindrance is pointed out well in *Fulfilled in Your Hearing:* "Since the homily is integrally related to the liturgy, and since liturgy presupposes a community that gathers to celebrate it, the homily is by definition related to a community. Homily services can be helpful in the interpretation of scriptural texts (though generally not as much as some basic exegetical resources) and give some ideas on how these texts can be related to contemporary human concerns. But they cannot provide individual preachers with specific indications of how these texts can be heard by the particular congregations to whom they will preach" (#58).

Homily services can help a preacher when the texts are concerned with a liturgical season like Advent, Lent, or Easter. They might help to develop the homily by providing good examples, stories, or illustrations. They should, however, never replace the hard work, sweat, reflection, and prayer needed to produce a homily suited for one's own community.

In a recent interview with Larry King, Billy Graham was asked if he had any regrets concerning his life. Billy responded, "Yes. I should have spent more time in study and prayer and less time in travel."

Homilies that deeply touch people's lives do not spout off the top of one's head. They arise from a deep sea of reflection.

Preparing a homily means living with the words of Scripture until they come alive, making connections with people's lives and one's own experience. We need to engage people in their everyday experience, as Jesus did. As one accomplished preacher exhorted: "Make Jesus the center of your preaching."

> An older priest who was known for his good homilies asked a younger priest, "How long do you spend preparing?"
>
> The young priest responded, "A couple of hours," and then proceeded to ask the older priest, "And how long do you spend?"
>
> The older priest replied, "Well, I start reading a book on Monday. I think about my homily every spare moment, make notes. Then on Saturday night I spend five or six hours writing it out word for word."

We preach a word that is powerful yet powerless. Even though God's word is as powerful as a two-edged sword, the assembly is free to reject it. Jesus's words were powerful because he spoke with authority, but some people would not accept his message. This same paradox demands total commitment from us in preparing our homilies.

4   BECOMING A PRAY-ER

> If preaching is prayer, then the preacher must be a pray-er. Not simply that you can count on me for X number of spiritual activities on any given day....My whole life must be a prayer. I mean, concretely, that the context, the setting, the framework of all I think and say and do should be a relationship of love with Father, Son, and Holy Spirit.

These powerful words of Walter Burghardt indeed represent a challenge for any preacher. The heart and center of preaching preparation is prayer. Preachers need to be rooted and grounded in prayer because, as George Herbert wrote, prayer is "God's breath...the soul's blood." Good preaching is preeminently a prayer event, and so, like prayer, is a religious experience. Both prayer and preaching enable individuals to delve more deeply into the gift of mystery, a gift not earned or merited, but often a surprise from a loving God.

Preachers would do well to ask themselves: Do we really know God? Do we really know Jesus? Too many preachers know the theology of God but not the God of theology. In finding God, preachers are challenged to lose their lives, to risk all to gain what Francis of Assisi called, "My God and my All." Francis discovered his all through prayer, as many of the saints did.

When I was a novice, I had the opportunity to listen to Solanus Casey, OFMCap, a simplex priest (one who is not allowed to hear confessions or preach). He had a very thin, wispy voice which was barely audible. But the audience was held spellbound by his words because we could sense that he was in deep communion with God. Fr. Casey spent many hours in prayer; this was reflected in both his life and in his speaking.

A relationship with Jesus

In his book *Intimacy with God,* Thomas Keating, OSB, writes, "Friendship with Christ has reached commitment when we decide to establish a life of prayer and a program for daily life tailored to getting closer to Christ and deeper into the Trinitarian life of love."

To be effective, every preacher needs to establish a life of prayer and a closer relationship to Christ. Jesus once asked his disciples: "Who do the crowds say that I am?" (Lk 9:18). This is the basic question preachers might repeatedly ask themselves in reference to prayer. Who is Jesus Christ in my life? What does he mean to me? How do we respond to Jesus' threefold question to Peter, "Do you love me more than these?" (Jn 21:15)?

Prayer is indispensable and fundamental to good preaching. It cannot be reduced to external regulations, like some cookbook recipe. Prayer has to become a priority for the preacher, as important as breathing is to our lives. What would happen to our preaching if preachers nourished themselves each day in contemplative prayer? How often has prayer become a last resort for some preachers?

Prayer, as well as preaching, demands a response. God continues to wait for our response, which often means to simply experience what God is doing in our midst. In prayer, as in liturgy, we praise God's love, mercy, forgiveness, and compassion. That is why preaching is such an intricate part of the liturgy. As the *Constitution on the Sacred Liturgy* states: "The homily, therefore, is to be highly esteemed as part of the liturgy itself." If word and sacrament are so intimately connected, it is the preacher's task to effect this. How better to achieve this than by deepening our prayer life?

If we are to proclaim the good news or speak for God, we need to be more than just good people with an array of virtues. We might be gifted communicators or possess a gift for words, but our union with God in prayer is far more important than our skills. A strong prayer life will deepen our faith, enabling us to trust that we will preach as Jesus did. This does not mean we have to be saints, or be perfect, only that we acknowledge our sinfulness as David did when the prophet Nathan confronted him with his sin (2 Sam 12:7).

If we have ceased to pray, we become like the barren fig tree that

Jesus cursed; we become like shriveled oranges with no juice. We might be able to hoodwink our listeners for a time, but eventually we dry up and become empty cisterns. Most people are rather perceptive, and can tell if we have prepared our homilies. They can also tell if we are prayerful preachers. For the message to be believable, the messenger should be believable. Francis of Assisi told his friars, "A preacher ought first in secret prayer to draw the water he intends later to pour out in sacred sermon; he ought to grow warm within before he utters cold words without."

Our own faith life

Alfred McBride, OPraem, insists that congregations are able to tell when a preacher is working at one's faith life or not. If the preacher isn't, McBride likens the listeners to sheep without a shepherd. Faith makes the preacher believable, and if the preacher is not believable neither is the message. We must always remember that Jesus is the message and we are the messengers.

Good preachers share their faith with others, addressing the listeners' faith experiences from a perspective of their own faith experiences. There is an interaction of our spirituality with the spirituality of our listeners. This spirituality can be compared to the matrix out of which our preaching arises. For example, Jesus preached much differently than the scribes and Pharisees; Paul's preaching is a departure from the four evangelists of his time.

Since a homily is a faith statement about our lives, it is an opportunity to help people praise and thank God. Walter Brueggemann states that proclamation is "a place where people come to receive new materials, or old materials freshly voiced, which will fund, feed, nurture, nourish, legitimate, and authorize a counterimagination of the world." Who is best suited to accept that challenge but the preacher of deep faith? Therefore, preachers should ask themselves: Does my homily leave the hearers closer to God than before?

As preachers we need to realize that we say more than what is actually said. If a preacher does not believe in the efficacy of the word, it will be conveyed in subtle but powerful ways: a lack of bodily gesture and proper intonation, but also with inadequate preparation.

Most listeners don't want to hear lofty theological speculation, heavy exegetical analysis, or oratorical flamboyance. Preachers don't have to be glib salespersons, witty entertainers, clever lawyers, or "princes of the pulpit." Most essential is that the preacher be a person of faith.

Preachers are invited to become gurus, defined as spiritual teachers, whose own behavior forms the basis for their preaching. And so preachers must practice what they preach. Once we have learned to integrate our behavior into our preaching we have a better chance of becoming a guru: we cannot give what we do not possess. Our life of faith and prayer act as a well from which we can draw living waters to nourish and quench the thirst of our listeners.

Is it any wonder why Jesus was so effective in his preaching? We often find him in prayer, especially in the gospel of Luke, where he is depicted in prayer more than fourteen times. In another gospel, Mark tells us that one day Jesus said to the apostles: "'Come away by yourselves to a deserted place and rest a while.' People were coming and going in such great numbers, and they had no opportunity to eat. So they went off in the boat by themselves to a deserted place" (6:31–32).

Many preachers need to heed that invitation more often to deepen their prayer lives. We too readily make excuses that we are too busy, or rationalize that there are more important matters that need our attention.

It is said that Thomas More got up at three in the morning to pray. (On hearing that, someone quipped, "We could get up at four.") For fifty-two years Fulton Sheen claimed that the secret to his preaching and teaching was his holy hour spent in prayer. Some of the most active saints in Christian tradition—like Thomas Aquinas, Augustine, Mother Cabrini, Vincent de Paul, and Mother Teresa of Calcutta—spent the most time in prayer. They found the time to pray despite their busy lives.

Dryness in prayer

At times, many of us experience dryness in prayer, as well as in our preaching. All creative people—and preachers are called upon to be creative people—experience desolation and agony. When this happens—when our minds become paralyzed, our ideas a maze of trivialities, and our speech a beating of the air—the tendency is to give up. Yet we cannot.

We must accept there will be dry times, occasions when we are completely devoid of any inspiration. Then, especially, we need to intensify our prayer and be open to how God is working in our lives. When John of the Cross and Teresa of Avila experienced these dark moments, they remained faithful in their prayer and became great mystics.

By praying with deep faith, we have the assurance that God will feed us no matter how dry and hungry we might feel. God fed the Israelites out in the desert. Elijah was fed by an angel, and with that food he was able to walk to Mount Horeb. Jesus fed the five thousand in the desert. And as he prayed in the garden of Gethsemane, Jesus was strengthened by an angel for "his sweat became like drops of blood falling on the ground" (Lk 22:44). We too are strengthened, fed, and nourished in a special way through prayer, often in ways unknown to us.

Praying over Scripture

People want to see the risen Christ in us, as Mary Magdalene did in the garden when she cried out, "Rabboni." Many of our listeners are like the disciples on the way to Emmaus; they are discouraged and disheartened by the trials and travesties of life. We need to break open the Scriptures for them as Jesus did for the disciples, so they can also say: "Were not our hearts burning within us while he was talking to us on the road, while he was opening the scriptures to us?" (Lk 24:32). We want to set the hearts of our listeners on fire with our words, which are the product of our prayer.

To help listeners see Christ in us we need to pray over the Scripture texts, first searching for how they apply to our own lives. We might be tempted to focus on our listeners, thinking: "Ah, this is good material for the lazy, the racists, the impatient, the resentful." Yet first we need to focus on ourselves; with the tax collector, we pray, "God, be merciful to me, a sinner!" (Lk 18:13).

Praying Scripture means to explore the events, characters, concrete images, and values that are found within the text. Prayer helps us to be more attentive to the conflicts and tensions that are often presented in the passages. As we delve into Scripture, we often arrive at a possible resolution. For example, we know the outcome of the story about Jesus' temptation in the desert. But when a preacher puts a twist on the story and presents it as the listener's threefold temptation, what is the outcome of the tension between possessions, power, and prestige?

The Scriptures should be interiorized by a preacher, and that can happen best through prayerful study and reflection. God's word then comes alive in us, allowing us to more easily convey the power of those words to our listeners. As Jerome once said, "When your head droops at night, let a page of Scripture pillow it."

We pray with Scripture to allow God to speak to us. God has spoken to our ancestors and now wants to speak to us. Are we ready to be guided by the Holy Spirit? Can we say with Abram, "Yes, Lord, I am ready"? Do we allow God to speak to us in a burning bush the way God spoke to Moses, or do we have all kinds of excuses and distractions? Recently, a retired priest confessed that one of the benefits of retirement is he can devote more time to his homilies. Another priest told me that he goes to his sister's home to get away from many distractions of his ministry so he can concentrate on his homily.

As we pray over Scripture, we might ask ourselves: What is it I want to preach about concerning the Scripture passages? What vital issue, tension, value, or relevant idea from this passage stands out in bold relief? Suppose we are meditating on the passage from Luke where Jesus calms the sea (8:22–25). Like Jonah in the boat as he tries to flee from God (Jon 1:1—2:10), Jesus is asleep in the boat with the apostles. When the sea rises up in a storm, Jesus rebukes it just as he rebuked unclean spirits. Yahweh also rebuked the sea during the flight of the Israelites from Egypt (Ex 14:8–30). Yahweh roared at the Red Sea and it dried up. And so, the point of our meditation might be this: if we don't feel God is paying attention to us (a common complaint) we might revisit the Scripture passages about Jonah, the exodus from Egypt, and the apostles in the boat with Jesus.

We can use an Ignatian approach to prayer and place ourselves in the biblical event. Here imagination plays an important role. As an example, let's consider the parable of the prodigal son. With whom do we identify in this story? Some of us will identify with the prodigal son or the loving father, and a few with the elder son. This son is the righteous one who remains faithful but will not rejoice at the reconciliation of the whole family. How often we see this scene repeated today.

For Ignatius, forming a decision in prayer was important. And so we can pray about how the story of the prodigal son might have ended. What did the elder son say or do to his younger brother? How did the prodigal son live out his repentance? We can take the point further by asking ourselves: What is our unfinished business? How do we live out this parable in our daily lives?

Listening to God

Listening is crucial to prayer. God speaks to us and asks us to listen. When God spoke to Samuel, he thought Eli was calling him. Finally, he recognized it was God and said, "Speak, Lord, for your servant is listening" (1 Sam 3:9). Terry Anderson, who was a prisoner in Lebanon for many years, stated, "It's easiest to hear God when we are stripped of pride and arrogance, when we have nothing to rely on except God."

To actively listen means to listen with your heart more than your head. Jesus actively listened to others and the Father, which explains why Jesus was such an effective preacher. When we actively listen, something within us has to die; as Jesus said, "Very truly, I tell you, unless a grain of wheat falls into the earth and dies, it remains just a single grain; but if it dies, it bears much fruit" (Jn 12:24).

Fulfilled in Your Hearing emphasizes the importance of listening: "Attentive listening to Scripture and to the people is, in essence, a form of prayer, perhaps the form of prayer most appropriate to the spirituality of the priest and the preacher. There is nothing more essential than prayerful listening for effective preaching, a praying over the texts which seeks the light and fire of the Holy Spirit to kindle the now meaning in our hearts" (#21).

Once we have listened to God's word and heard God speaking to us through others, we need to interiorize that word. Then it can have life-giving meaning to our proclamation, and listeners will profit more from our prayerful reflections.

Praying with the senses

When we preach, it is important to appeal to the senses. And so we must learn to pray in a way that involves our senses, too. Experts point out that people basically learn in three different ways The first group learns mainly through sight, and sixty percent of the population is visually oriented. So when we pray over Scripture we should ask: What do I see? What kind of pictures? What are the shadows, lights, or darknesses present? Let's take the Easter passage from Luke (24:1–12). When the women came to the tomb, it was early dawn, still dark; maybe some stars could still be seen. What did they see on the way there?

Another passage rich in visual texture is the story of Dives and Lazarus (Lk 16:19–31). One might picture the sharp and noticeable contrast between Dives (which means "rich man" in the Vulgate) and Lazarus. We see Dives entertaining in style and dressing elegantly, while Lazarus, an emaciated beggar covered with sores and filth, lies outside the gate. We might then take the image one step further in our prayer and ask: Who is Dives or Lazarus in my community, in my parish, or in the marketplace? Is there a little of Dives and Lazarus in me?

The second group learns mainly through hearing or listening. They are attuned to God's call or hearing God's word in a meaningful way. About thirty percent of all people learn in this way. And so, what do we hear when we pray Scripture? What are the sounds? Are they loud or soft, pleasant or raucous? When the women approached the tomb on that resurrection morning, did they hear the roosters crowing? Did they whimper because they did not know who was going to roll away the stone? As I listen to the Dives and Lazarus story, how do I hear the difference between the two? What is the sound of Abraham rejecting Dives's pleas?

The third group learns mainly through feeling, either kinesthetically or emotionally. About ten percent of all people learn through this method. They relate to words such as sense, feel, or grasp, and emotions like fear, joy, anger, and sadness. When praying this way we want to feel God's presence, and experience whatever emotions may arise. These feelings can then be conveyed to our listeners to help them feel that same presence of God. So we might ask as we pray: How did the women feel as they approached the tomb? What did they sense was going to happen? What emotion stood out for them in bold relief? In the story of Dives and Lazarus, we can examine how we feel about the outcome of the story. Do we sense that justice has been served?

Praying with our senses might seem laborious to some preachers. But by addressing each of the sense orientations in our own prayer, we can better relate to the learning processes of our listeners. Experts point out that listeners respond in a positive manner when they are reached on a level of the senses. Seeing, hearing, and feeling the action is a very effective way to preach God's word, and praying in this way will facilitate the process.

Prayer is at the heart and center of our preparation. The goal of most devout Muslims is to blend the Koran with their thoughts and actions, so they become living Korans. If preachers blend the gospel into their lives and actions, they too become a living metaphor of the gospels.

When prayer is at the heart and center of our lives, we are like Jeremiah (20:9): "If I say, 'I will not mention him, or speak any more in his name,' then within me there is something like a burning fire shut up in my bones; I am weary with holding it in, and I cannot."

5   LIGHTING A FIRE

There is an urgent need today for passionate preaching. The more preachers have prepared and prayed Scripture, the more we should be able to preach God's Word with passion.

Preachers don't have to envision themselves as another Demosthenes or a thundering prophet. If we devote ourselves to the task of preaching with love, it will be evident to the hearers. People will comment, "You like what you're doing, don't you?" If we are bored or lazy with this important task, our preaching will be boring and lifeless. Preaching that is impregnated with love will energize our words and delivery; a lifeless preacher will only encourage a lifeless community.

Gideon considered himself the lowest man in the tribe and unworthy to lead the Israelites against the Midianites. But God assured Gideon that God would be with him. Jeremiah considered himself too young, while Isaiah protested that he had unclean lips. Yet God gave Jeremiah the ability to proclaim his message forcefully; God cleansed the lips of Isaiah. Why would we expect that God would not do the same for any preacher?

The very nature of good preaching is prophetic, passionate, and challenging, and so it must impart enthusiasm, power, and joy. (By the way, the root of the word "enthusiasm" means to be "inspired by God.") Ralph Waldo Emerson once said, "Nothing great was ever accomplished without enthusiasm," and this is certainly true of preaching. Too many people in our assemblies are left hungry or spiritually anemic by listless preaching. Homilies are not meant to be sleeping pills.

In addressing a gathering of priests, Archbishop Daniel Pilarczyk of Cincinnati said: "Like all good teachers, the priest also needs to be interested in and enthusiastic about what he teaches." He went on to say that this calls for "the deep seated conviction that what is being taught here is authentically important."

Jesus said, "I came to bring fire to the earth, and how I wish it were already kindled!" (Lk 12:49). Every preacher needs to enkindle that fire within oneself and then share the power with others. To use the phrase popularized by author Sam Keen, we must have a "fire in the belly!" We have to let the gospel message pulse throughout our whole being. If we are not aflame, we approach the pulpit as if with leg chains wrapped around our ankles.

Jesus held people spellbound by his preaching because he spoke with authority and power. People followed him around, glued to every word he said. This is certainly a far cry from the people who rush to get out of church, or who become impatient if the homily takes longer than usual. As Catherine de Hueck stated, "The moment you start preaching like Jesus Christ preached, the world comes around you and immediately keeps on following you."

We preachers also need to be anointed with the fire of the Holy Spirit. Walter Burghardt insists that, "If our homilies are to inspire as well as inform, our preachers must be set aflame." The Pentecostals and evangelicals use the term "anointed" preaching, which means that the preacher is gifted with the Holy Spirit, and conveys that same Spirit to the listeners. Preachers endowed with this gift put forth a simple yet profound message animated by the Spirit.

Unless we open ourselves up to the Holy Spirit, our preaching will lack the force and energy needed today to touch people's lives. Jesus went into the synagogue and unrolled the scroll of Isaiah and read, "The Spirit of the Lord is upon me, because he has anointed me to bring good news to the poor" (Lk 4:18). John the Baptist, a great preacher, received the power of the Holy Spirit when he was still within his mother's womb. That same Spirit can touch us too if we are open and willing to accept this grace.

In writing to the people of Corinth, Paul said, "My speech and my proclamation were not with plausible words of wisdom, but with a demonstration of the Spirit and of power, so that your faith might rest not on human wisdom but on the power of God" (1 Cor 2:4–5). And Karl Rahner stated that preaching is not about new information or clarity of doctrine, but rather to awaken hearers to the wonder of life and mystery as well as the presence and power of the Spirit in their lives.

The passionate preacher has something to say. Preachers must commit themselves to energize others who hear the good news, because this might be the only good news they hear. If hearers are not enthusiastic about God's word after hearing our preaching, then we have failed.

The efficacy of God's word

Before preachers can change others, they might have to change themselves. True preachers can always be known by the way they share their lives with others, a life passed through the "fire of thought." If the power of God's word has not gripped them, it won't grip their hearers. Preaching without emotional involvement in God's word is usually dead.

The word itself is imbued with power. Thomas Aquinas wrote, "Even the words of the gospel are not gospel." In the final analysis, the gospel is the gift of the Spirit, but good preachers can enhance the efficacy of the word by a lively proclamation. Yet something must happen to preachers before they can proclaim the message forcefully. Jeremiah endured an interior crisis of being duped, mocked, and made an object of derision before he became a great prophet. Preachers need to "feel fiercely" as Rabbi Abraham Joshua Heschel once said.

Some preachers are afraid of what God might ask of them. The more they contemplate Scripture, the more they realize the real challenge in living out God's word. Each preacher must go through a conversion, followed by an inversion, and then an immersion into the power of God's word. This is the process known as metanoia.

Paul was a great persecutor of the early Christian church. But when he encountered God along the road to Jerusalem, he became one of the greatest preachers the church has ever known. A similar type of conversion is also demanded of every preacher. After his experience, Paul continued to immerse himself more into Jesus Christ and the paschal mystery. We need to imitate Paul in this regard by immersing ourselves in Jesus Christ and in the power of God's word. As Paul states, "So faith comes from what is heard, and what is heard comes through the word of Christ" (Rom 10:17).

Preaching from the heart

Good preachers speak from their hearts as well as their heads; as a result they preach with more compassion and animation. One might object, saying: "I don't want to be emotional." Yet there are far too many laid-back homilies because the preacher fears being too theatrical, artificial, dramatic, or emotional. It is much easier to tone down emotion or enthusiasm than vice versa.

Like a good pianist blending together the eighty-eight keys on their instrument, vibrant and alive preachers try to blend in a wide emotional range in proclaiming the good news. Charles Laughton once wrote that "good reading is reading something you love to someone you love." Good preaching might be characterized in a similar way. Good preachers don't bludgeon the hearers, but nudge them, helping them feel closer to God and know who Jesus is.

Preachers don't need the persuasive logic of a lawyer, the cogent reasoning of a scientist, or the Cartesian clarity of a philosopher; but we do need more heart to heart preaching. As Demosthenes once said of his archrival, Aeschines, "When you orate, they say, 'How well he speaks.' When I orate, they say, 'Let us march against Philip.'"

A famous Southern Baptist preacher once said this about his homilies: "Well, first I reads myself full. Then I thinks myself clear. Then I prays myself hot. And then I lets myself go!" Many experts agree that hearers are influenced more by the manner of presentation than the arguments or examples used. In *Preaching the Just Word,* Walter Burghardt wrote, "Our people should sense from our words and our faces, from our gestures and our whole posture, that we love the crucified communities with a crucifying passion, that we agonize over the hardness of our hearts, our ability to 'eat, drink, and be merry,' while a billion humans go to bed hungry; that the heavy-burdened can look to us not so much for answers as for empathy, for compassion."

Few of us, if any, will be called upon to preach the way Archbishop Oscar Romero did. He told his people, "This holy Mass, this Eucharist is clearly an act of faith. The body broken and blood shed for human beings encourage us to give our body and blood up to suffering and pain, as Christ did—not for self, but to bring justice and peace to people. Let us be intimately united in faith and hope at this moment." After speaking these moving words, he was shot to death, his fate undoubtedly sealed in part by the powerful Christian conviction expressed in his homilies.

Back in the early 1990s, Martin Jenco, a Servite priest, spoke about his kidnaping and imprisonment in Beirut. He based his talk on the life of Jeremiah. Fr. Jenco read his talk very carefully, word for word, in an urgent, impassioned voice. His eyes and countenance glistened with strong conviction. He mesmerized his listeners.

All of us remember Martin Luther King, Jr.'s, famous sermon, popularly known as "I Have a Dream": "...and when we allow freedom to ring, when we let it ring from every village and every hamlet, from every state and every city, we will be able to speed up that day when all God's children, Black men and White men, Jews and Gentiles, Protestants and Catholics, will be able to join hands and be, in the words of the old Negro spiritual: 'Free at last. Free at last. Thank God Almighty, we are free at last.'"

Good feedback

Good feedback from our hearers is most beneficial for most preachers. When people tell us how much they appreciated our preaching, it is an incentive for us to commit ourselves more intensely to passionately communicate the good news.

A fine compliment after a homily is, "That message really spoke to me," or, "I felt as if you were speaking right to me." We know then that what was proclaimed had an effect. (At one time in my life, I felt that people were just being kind to me when they complimented my preaching. I have since changed my thinking and realized how sincere people are in their compliments. Their words, I know, have helped me become a better preacher.)

Clarence Williams, CPPS, a gifted and passionate preacher, said that the greatest "shot in the arm" he received concerning his preaching was a telephone call he got from a parishioner after a funeral at which he presided. The person said, "Father, your homily at the funeral today was beautiful. When I die, I want you to preach at my funeral. No matter where you are, you will be sent for."

William Graham, a communications expert, insists that the greatest single obstacle to effective communication is a preacher's poor self-image, and suggests that preachers develop their own personal potential. Likewise, Dean Hoge of Catholic University discovered that self-esteem was the preacher's number one concern. And Frank McNulty, a priest in the Archdiocese of Newark, maintains that "the self-esteem problem of priests is linked to good preaching. It seems that better preachers get more affirmation and that increases self-esteem."

Like John the Baptist, preachers prepare the way of the Lord, and make straight his paths. We proclaim, "The time is fulfilled, and the kingdom of God has come near; repent, and believe in the good news" (Mk 1:15). Soon after Jesus uttered these same words, his first disciples left their fishing boats and nets, and followed him. This is the power of passionate preaching.

6   CREATIVITY

When was the last time you heard—or gave—a homily that was imaginative or creative? This chapter will suggest some ideas on how to be more creative in proclaiming the word of God.

What does it mean to be creative? It means to approach an idea, situation, or problem in a novel way by introducing some new insight, stimulating the imagination, or developing new meaning within an idea. In Walter Burghardt's opinion, the most serious trouble with preaching is a lack of imagination. He says, "We preachers approach the pulpit with all the imagination of a dead fish." A preacher needs to be willing to explore new ideas and experiences.

Imagination is our gift for creating images. Not every preacher has an active imagination, but every good preacher needs one. Burghardt defines imagination as "the capacity we all have to make the material an image of the immaterial or spiritual. It is a creative power."

Imaginative preaching springs from what Wordsworth called "emotion recollected in tranquility." Imaginative preaching helps to look at the present so we can shape the future. It means to be in touch with common human experiences like life, death, sex, love, violence, racism—and God. Imaginative preaching is a conduit for expressing old ideas in a new and fresh way.

Let's use the analogy of a photographer approaching a picture opportunity. In our homily, we can apply a wide-angle lens to some Scripture text, relying on our intuition to help develop the message, and be surprised with the results. Or, a preacher can zoom in on a text with a telephoto lens, focusing on one specific area or problem.

Creative preaching strives to free one from restraints, allowing for a much broader way to approach a text. We might recall Abraham's response to God's call here, as noted in the epistle to the Hebrews: "By faith Abraham obeyed when he was called to set out for a place that he was to receive as an inheritance; and he set out, not knowing where he was going" (11:8). Like Abraham, God calls us to places we would rather not go; we must learn to walk where there is no road. The key is an openness to how and where the Spirit guides us.

On the other hand, a preacher has to guard against aimless wandering, like the Israelites in the desert who often forgot where they were going and what God had promised them. How do we harmonize an openness to the Spirit with a particular Scripture text? We must first ask ourselves: What is the main thrust of the passage or passages? (Here we do well to choose one point of view, and not try to tie all three readings together.)

After reading and praying over the texts, one might brainstorm and jot down any ideas that come to mind—even if they sound crazy or weird. Once the ideas are there on paper, evaluate them for their practicality or usefulness. Trust your own instincts; too many preachers resort to homily hints or pre-packaged homilies rather than trust their own ideas. This approach can short-circuit the creative process. Don't ever stop your flow of ideas; you can always separate the wheat from the chaff along the way.

The introduction

Creativity starts with the introduction to your homily. What do you think the reaction of an assembly is to a phrase such as, "In today's gospel, we see Jesus..." or some similarly worn-thin sentence? Consider this creative introduction to a homily on the Scripture passage "Come to me, all you that are weary and are carrying heavy burdens, and I will give you rest" (Mt 11:28):

> One day a man came to a preacher and said, "Oh, these problems, I wish I could go where there are no problems." The preacher responded, "Why, I was just in such a place. This afternoon I conducted a funeral, and now I'm returning from the

cemetery. People out there are not under any stress."

You can be sure the assembly paid attention after that introduction! Also try opening with a strong quote, such as this one from statesman and author Dag Hammarskjöld: "The longest journey is the journey within." Your homily might then focus on how hard it is to accept our powerlessness, and how many of us long to take flight from our inner struggles. Another technique is to use a headline from the today's newspaper, one that will inevitably catch the ear of your listeners.

A penetrating question can often prompt interesting results. One preacher asked "How many of you consider yourselves Catholic?" Most of the people in the pews that day raised their hands. He then continued by talking about what it means to be a Catholic today: "Love your enemies, do good to those who hate you, bless those who curse you, pray for those who abuse you" (Lk 6:27–28). This preacher concluded his homily by asking, "*Now* how many of us can say we are Catholics?"

Many provocative questions can be found in Scripture: God asked of Adam and Eve, "What is this that you have done?" (Gen 3:13); "Who do people say that I am?" (Mk 8:27); and "Simon son of John, do you love me more than these?" (Jn 21:15). These questions can lead us to reflect on the everyday questions that people may be asking in their own lives: "How can I forgive him after what he did to me?" Or, "Why do I have to suffer so much?"

A piece of poetry can set the tone of a homily. Storyteller and author John Shea used this poem in a homily on the resurrection and the stone covering the tomb:

> So
> if a passer-by would ask
> who rules this life,
> point him to this stone
> and tell him I am inside
> disassembling the handiwork of
> God.

In his essay entitled, "Priest as Poet," Karl Rahner wrote: "To the poet is entrusted the word." Poets paint pictures using good images. They are able to see what we don't see. They fathom the ambiguities of life and explain them by means of similes, metaphors, and analogies that can inspire us to a deeper vision of life.

One might also start a homily with a paradoxical statement, like this one from Meister Eckhart: "I pray God to free me of God." Jesus himself used many paradoxes to get across his point, especially when he spoke about discipleship: "For those who want to save their life will lose it, and those who lose their life for my sake will save it" (Lk 9:24).

Theologian Paul Tillich insisted that there is no communication where there is no participation. In light of this statement, one form of creative preaching is using a dialogue homily. Although this approach can get unwieldy in a large assembly, it can be an effective way to reflect on the gospel in smaller Sunday or weekday gatherings. Here, the creative challenge is to make preaching participative, which is not the normal course for a preacher. One must involve the person in the pew.

Victor Capriolo, a priest of the Archdiocese of Milwaukee, began one of his homilies on prejudice by asking the congregation to imagine that all parishes had been told to implement the following policy: "Bald people are prohibited from occupying the first ten pews in the front of the church. Months of clinical research has provided conclusive evidence that bald people are definitely more immoral, less intelligent, and are generally less desirable socially than people with a full head of hair. Out of reverence for the sacred, therefore, we must insist that bald people keep the above-stated distance from the sanctuary." With this dramatic statement, Capriolo was able to involve his listeners in a spirited homily about the ridiculousness of prejudice.

In order to engage our listeners, we should know what is going on in their lives. We should be aware of their pains, struggles, doubts, fears, hurts, sorrows, and joys. Likewise, we must be willing to share the trials and tribulations of our own lives; the marks of authentic pain should identify the preacher. Jesus was willing to show his disciples the wounds in his hands and his side. What are we willing to show our listeners? As the Roman poet Horace once said, "If you want me to weep, you must weep yourself."

Illustrating the homily

We are a visual and electronic culture, and using this to our advantage will make our homilies more effective. How do we build a bridge over the chasm separating our world of preaching from our world of mass media? How do we integrate the various media in communicating God's word?

One way is by observing the techniques that mass media use to appeal to the audience. For example, did you ever notice how television commercials start off with something catchy, trying to capture our attention? An ad for a headache remedy might start with a question: Do you have a headache? This will be followed by a proposal: Do you want to get rid of the headache? Then we are given the answer to the need: aspirin or Tylenol or another pain reliever. This is followed by proof: the product has worked! Finally, there is a call for action: buy this product now. Preachers too can well use these simple steps in constructing a homily.

Using visual aids can be another effective way to convey a gospel message. We don't have to get "high tech" with our visuals, rather, we can stick with everyday objects. A match can be used to point out the potential for good or bad, just as each person has the potential for good or bad. A match can be used in a positive way, to light a warming fire or a gas stove for cooking. Yet a match can cause great destruction when used carelessly. In the same way, we too can use our human potential for good or bad. Once the match is lit it becomes a tiny, glorious flame, a reminder of how Jesus challenged us to be "the light of the world" (Mt 5:14).

A piece of tapestry might be used to make a point about the mystery of our lives. Hold up the cloth, showing the backside, a jumble of interwoven pieces of thread. This is what our lives often seem like as we journey through them and encounter events that don't make much sense at the time. But once the tapestry is turned around, a beautiful pattern can be seen. This might be our experience at a certain point, when we start to see all the events and circumstances of our lives coming together to form a beautiful pattern.

Many other aids can be used. I once used a scroll to preach about the time Jesus went into the synagogue at Nazareth, and was himself offered a scroll. As you recall, he opened it to the passage from Isaiah, "The Spirit of the Lord is upon me, because he has anointed me to bring good news to the poor. He has sent me to proclaim release to the captives and recovery of sight to the blind, to let the oppressed go free, to proclaim the year of the Lord's favor" (Lk 4:18–19). At the appropriate time I opened the scroll and read the full passage. At the end of the homily, I asked those people who wanted to commit themselves to being spirited and animated people, willing to bring glad tidings to others, to come forward and sign the scroll. This was brought up to the altar during the presentation of gifts.

Some preachers enhance their homilies by means of song. Pat Boone used to shake hands with as many people in his audience as possible, and then sing songs to bolster his gospel message. Jeff Vanden Heavel, a priest of the Green Bay diocese, has produced a number of tapes entitled, *Singing the Stories of the Good News*. He has become a very popular homilist. A classmate of mine, Ellis Zimmer, will often conclude a homily or talk with these words, "This reminds me of a song"—and then proceed to sing one. Songs have the power to emphasize a point, sometimes more effectively than words.

Homily aids that are used prudently, selectively, and with variation not only enhance a homily but help listeners to remember, recall, and better understand the message. So take up your media bag and preach. Rifle through the depths of your creative imagination, and follow in the footsteps of Jesus, the most creative preacher ever known.

7 GOOD IMAGERY

If we want someone to really enjoy a filet mignon, we let the person smell it, taste it, and savor it. If we are preaching about the Holocaust, we don't just say that six million Jews were exterminated. We try to help the assembly hear the roar of the gas ovens and see the mountains of bones.

One way to talk about mystery is to use imagery. Jesus did this well, and used many images and parables to describe the reign of God. Shakespeare often used metaphors to describe life, calling it a walking shadow, a poor player, or a tale told by an idiot.

Images can be like a many-faceted diamond, displaying different aspects of its richness, or like a prism revealing different colors. Images evoke a strong response from our listeners because of their innate appeal. Experts agree that the more powerful the sense image, the more powerful an idea that takes hold. Hearing someone say, "I love you" can't compare to a tender embrace.

The use of imagery has to become the warp and woof of our preaching, giving it life and meaning. Preachers can't throw a bagful of words at hearers, hoping that some of the words will hit and awaken the assembly. What salt can do for food, good imagery can do for preaching. If we are to be the salt of the earth, as Jesus encouraged us, we call forth the best in others. We need to "flavor" or enhance the lives of others by affirming them.

Good imagery appeals to the visual, tactile, and auditory dimensions of our world. Good imagery is multidimensional and open-ended, which can cause tension with, unsettle, or transform our listeners. Walter Brueggemann states that people don't change because of doctrinal argument or moral appeal. People change, he insists, "by the offer of new models, images, and pictures of how the pieces of life fit together."

Images are often used to explain something that is complicated or unclear. The clearer the image the sharper the meaning or explanation. Choosing a good image demands imagination and hard work.

Scriptural imagery

The Scriptures are filled with imagery. James A. Wallace believes that "biblical imagery can also function in the consciousness of the community of believers, getting into their hearts and heads, into their dreams and hopes, stirring up things and resulting in an increasing realization in the world of the community's self identity as being in Christ and commitment to his mission."

One of the most vivid and frequently used images for God is a rock, particularly in the books of Deuteronomy, Samuel, and Isaiah, as well as in the Psalms. This image has the ability to make our hearers aware of God as their stability, power, eternity, and place of refuge. It also symbolizes God's enduring love and protection, which call us to greater dependence and faith in God. But we must remember that any image of God is inadequate, as God transcends all images.

The Book of Revelation is jam-packed with images: the four horsemen, the lamb's book of life; the woman clothed with the sun, the moon at her feet and her head crowned with stars; the seven-headed dragon; God seated on a heavenly throne, surrounded by angels playing their harps, just to mention a few. (Passages from this book are seldom read at Sunday liturgy, but many of its enduring images can be found in hymns and spirituals.)

Jesus himself is the ultimate image of God's love and glory. During his three years of ministry, he proclaimed the good news by means of concrete and precise images. One such image is found in the gospel of Matthew (23:37), where Jesus says: "Jerusalem, Jerusalem, the city that kills the prophets and stones those who are sent to it! How often have I desired to gather your children together as a hen gathers her brood under her wings, and you were not willing!" All of his listeners had actually seen a hen nervously gathering her chicks to protect them from danger. And so they could well see themselves as the foolish chicks who had wandered away, and see how their loving God longed to bring them back into the fold.

Jesus used many other images when he spoke to people. He compared the reign of God to a farmer scattering seed in his field (Mk 4:3–9), to convey the idea that growth and harvest are not dependent on the farmer, but on God. He compared the kingdom of God to a mustard seed, a pearl of great price, yeast in the dough, and a net thrown into the water (Mt 13:31–33, 44–50). These were all images that were familiar to the people of his time. Jesus called himself the light of the world (Jn 8:12), one who dispels the darkness of life. This was a powerful example for a culture that did not know electricity, and relied on relatively few sources—the sun, fire, and oil lamps—for light.

Common images

Although most of the images used in Scripture were common to the people of those times, they are not always familiar to readers today. This can present a real challenge to the preacher. One good example is the image of the shepherd, which Jesus used to describe himself. Very few people today have actually seen a shepherd, or know what it is they really do. One suggestion is to take another image more common to our listeners, like a scoutmaster or a school principal, and use that as an analogy. An image that is rooted in the audience's experience will often prove more effective than one that is not.

On the other hand, the image of a good shepherd meant much to the late Joseph Cardinal Bernardin, who wrote in his book, *The Gift of Peace:* "The Good Shepherd, the model for all my ministry, is one who lays down his life for his people. Some live this calling literally, shedding their blood as martyrs. Others live it in the unstinting giving of their time, their energy, their very selves to those they have been called to serve. Whatever the future holds for me, I pledge this day to live as a good shepherd who willingly lays down his life for you."

Another image that can be used when speaking about leadership and ministry is that of a flock of geese flying in a V formation. By flying this way, they increase their flying range by seventy-one percent, a far greater distance than would be possible if each goose flew alone. When the lead goose tires, it rotates to the back of the V and allows another goose to take the front position. This example can be used to stress the importance of community and of working together to reach a goal. It also shows that we need to take turns being leaders, and doing the hard tasks.

I once heard Paul Wachdorf, a spiritual director at Mundelein Seminary in Chicago, use an example of the spacecraft Magellan to show how we hunger for God. This spacecraft, as you might recall, traveled to Venus some years ago to accurately map its surface. A few days after its arrival on the planet, however, mission control lost contact with Magellan. Fortunately, the designers of the spacecraft had built a search program into it, which enabled mission control to fix the problem from earth, allowing Magellan to complete its purpose. Wachdorf then spoke about how God has given us an innate search program to help us along our journey toward God.

Many of the documents from the Second Vatican Council contain well-known images: the church as the people of God, the family as the domestic church, other Christians as separated brethren. Less well-known images are of the laity as animators of our society, and worshipers who are not strangers or silent spectators. Robert Kinast, director of the Center for Theological Reflection, states: "These images stimulate our spiritual imagination and give us fresh ways to think about and enact our faith."

Hans Urs von Balthasar, a Swiss theologian, used musical imagery when he described the church as "playing her chords of love." He conceived Christianity as a great symphony whose melody has to be heard in such a way as to transcend any particular rendition. He explored revelation as a drama, an exhilarating love story where God's irresistible love would track down any sinner, even in hell's darkest corner.

Joseph Manton, CSSR, used very forceful imagery when he described death: "If Death were only the blunt end of a Dead-End street; if Death were only the tiny black period at the end of a sentence of life, with no page to follow, then every grave would be no more than a king-sized ashtray, and every headstone a monument to futile despair." Fulton Sheen described the Risen Christ in this way: "We need the Risen Jesus of the Scars for our times! The only language we speak today is 'blood, sweat, and tears.' A God without scars cannot understand our times." How true are these words, even today.

To end this chapter, here's a creative interpretation of a familiar parable (Mt 21:28–31):

> A man had a vineyard in the Napa Valley that had just been attacked by fungus. So, he went to his son and said, "Chablis, will you help me in the vineyard?" Chablis answered, "Yes, of course." But Chablis, distracted by friends, got into his red sports car, drove to San Francisco, and was never heard from again.
>
> The man then went to his other son. "Zinfandel, will you help me in the vineyard?" Zinfandel replied: "No, I'm busy." But as Zinfandel walked away, he had second thoughts (long pause). And so he returned and worked in his father's vineyard.
>
> God is our "second thoughts." God is in those brief moments before we decide or act. So, when you are in the store this week choosing a wine for dinner, ask yourself: When the temptations swirl around me, will it be chablis or (long pause) zinfandel?

8   SIMPLE LANGUAGE

Preachers often compete with squealing babies, latecomers, watch alarms, beepers, and people who are disinterested, distracted, or distressed. Now we even have to worry about cell phones ringing during Mass! All of these things are hard to prevent.

One thing a preacher can prevent is the all-too-common tendency to use language that is complicated. This type of preaching elicits comments such as: "That homily went right over my head," or "I had absolutely no idea what the preacher was talking about." Simplicity in language is of the utmost importance for a preacher to be effective. In a recent study conducted in one of the archdioceses in the United States, respondents overall ranked their pastor's ability to preach down-to-earth sermons as twentieth among twenty-four qualities.

Essentially, simplicity in language means using basic, common words to present your message, language that is easily understood by the people in the pews. It means that the preacher conveys one's thoughts so plainly that the listeners immediately understand what is being proclaimed. In his book, *How to Make Us Want Your Sermon,* Brian Atkinson writes: "Simple style comes from the love of the common words, the keen desire to use them, and the lasting effort to use them well."

In his ninth chapter of the Rule, Francis of Assisi asked his followers to preach with language that is "well considered and simple." He uttered a plea for preparation, both long-range and short-range. Long-range preparation meant prayer and study; short-range preparation implied that the preacher work out each homily carefully, with an emphasis on using simple language. Francis wanted his followers to be popular preachers who could speak in an intelligible and profitable way to the people, a way that could bring repentance, hope, and peace to others. He desired that preaching be "for the benefit and edification of the people."

Down through the years, every voice raised on the subject has insisted on the same thing: simplicity of language in preaching. The Council of Trent commanded priests to preach in a style accommodated to the capacity of their flocks. Pope Pius XII asked the priests of his diocese to "preach with simplicity....It is not scintillating and learned fluency that conquers souls, especially today, but rather the word of conviction that comes from the heart and goes to the heart." Pope John XXIII once bemoaned homiletic abstractions and profundities in an address made during his papacy.

Paul said it well when he wrote, in his first letter to the Corinthians (14:9): "So with yourselves; if in a tongue you utter speech that is not intelligible, how will anyone know what is being said? For you will be speaking into the air." It is only the language of ordinary life–simple, rustic language–that can reach the heart and mind. Ivory-tower talk may tickle the ear. But as Canon Drinkwater suggests, this kind of language "seals off the heart as effectively as trouble in the fuse box shuts off the electric current."

Herbert Spencer compared language to a mechanical apparatus. He stated that "whatever force is absorbed by the machine is deducted from the result." This meant that the more energy an audience has to expend trying to understand the words of a preacher, the less time and attention they can devote to the thought or idea. Baffling words act like friction; they deduct from the preacher's efficiency. Listeners will "spend too much mental power trying to clear away the obscurity, attempting to get down to the thought." And in the process they become exhausted by the time they get there–if they ever do.

How can one achieve simplicity in language, or improve upon this in a homily? Are there ways preacher might make one's homily more simple and understandable? The following list is not exhaustive, but does offer a few ways to make our preaching more simple.

"Think simple"

If we preachers are to preach simply, we need to think simply, with common words. Most of us have a stock of words that we employ when we think and talk. We also have a reservoir of words that we rarely use but understand. A preacher can effect a simple style by acquainting oneself with as many common words as possible, knowing exactly what they mean and then turning them correctly into homespun thought.

We can go back to the gospels and the simple language used by Jesus to convey a powerful message. Preachers should not be known for their mastery of English—or any other language, for that matter. Rather, they should be known for their ability to convey the good news to their listeners so the assembly can easily follow and understand the message. Some homilies may win much admiration and even be applauded by listeners, but all this is for naught if the listeners did not understand what the preacher was trying to get across.

Augustine wrote: "I prefer that grammarians should criticize me rather than that my people should not understand me." He adds by an ingenious comparison, "What is the value to me of a key of gold if it does not open the door I wish, or what is the harm of a wooden one if it does?"

One might test how well a homily has reached the hearts of the listeners by asking a few people: "Can you sum up the homily in one sentence?" If the summary needs several sentences, it probably was not simple.

Simple words

Simple language uses simple words. I've heard these words used in homilies before: efficacy, valid, licit, assiduity, revivification, and promulgation. Now, a well-educated audience might appreciate and understand this kind of language. The average audience sitting in the pews on Sunday, however, is a mixed group, with the poorly educated sitting next to the highly educated, and many others with an average education in between. Some experts recommend that the homily be addressed to the understanding of a twelve year old.

Avoid using big words, especially of Latin and Greek origin; simplicity of language demands the use of Anglo-Saxon or Norman French words. Here is a good example of a sentence that uses a lot of sophisticated language: The rustic intelligence cannot comprehend the scintillation of stellar luminaries or the stellar orbit. What does this mean in plain English? The peasant's mind can not grasp the twinkling of the stars or the sun's rounds in the sky.

Imagine that a father were to take a pork chop, smell it, and look disgusted. His little boy might say, "What's the matter with it, Pop?" The father answers, "It is undergoing a process of decomposition in the formation of new chemical compounds." The boy would probably say "Huh?" But if the father were to answer, "It's rotten," then the boy might easily hold his nose.

Words like " lugubrious," "mystical," "omniscience," "eschatological," and "transubstantiation" are nothing but show-stoppers, verbal blockades between the preacher and listener. If preachers persist in using this baffling approach, the listeners will certainly remain strangers; the preacher is moving along one orbit while the person in the pew is in another. Augustine wrote that it is useless to raise one's voice if we do not speak so we can be understood.

Does this mean that a preacher has to forgo sublime thought and beauty of expression? We can find the answer to this question in the Bible itself, which is, for the most part, a model of simplicity. One powerful example is the prologue to John's gospel, which opens with thoughts that are sublime, expressed in words that are simple and clear. The first three hundred words of this prologue include two hundred and fifty-eight words of one syllable. It is truly a masterpiece of simple language.

Consider this passage from a homily on creation, given by Walter Burghardt: "All this was born of God. Earth, sea, and sky, as we know them, are the fruits of a glorious adventure. Each flower, each cloud, each mountain range goes back in time to some nameless, perhaps shapeless, certainly mysterious matter that is significant for an unforgettable reason: it was shaped by God." These are basic thoughts and simple language, yet this passage is powerfully sublime.

If preachers have a choice between long words and short words, it is usually better to choose the shorter word. Sometimes, however, this is not helpful. For example, the word "fey" is short; it means fated to die or doomed. But how many people would know the meaning of this word if it were used in a homily? Therefore, we cannot make an absolute rule about choosing a short word unless stated in this way: choose the short word in preference to the long word, provided it is understood by the listeners.

As Mary Catherine Hilkert, OP, stated at a lecture I once attended, "Once you have said it, you have said it." What most often stops the listener is not the grandeur or sublimity of the thought, but the unfamiliar wording of the thought.

Sentence structure

In his "Letter on Preaching," Francis de Sales warned the Archbishop of Bourges to beware of long and involved sentences. This warning can apply to all preachers, as well. Long, involved sentences, even when printed, can challenge the most trained interpreters.

Notice the simple sentences in this homily on purgatory, written by Walter Burghardt: "The first question, therefore: is there such a thing as purgatory? Be realistic. Some day–perhaps today, perhaps thirty years from today–you will die. One hundred and forty thousand do each day. What will happen to you? This. Your soul will leave your body. That body will return to the earth from which it came."

Short sentences like these are much easier to deliver and often greatly enhance audience contact. Sentences cluttered with many phrases and clauses are far more difficult to comprehend or follow. Some of Cardinal Newman's long, involved sentences can bog us down, or make us reach for some Tylenol. One of the shortest sentences in the gospels, and one with the deepest meaning, is: "Jesus began to weep" (Jn 11:35).

If the thought expressed in a homily is easy to understand, the attention of the listeners will be centered on what is said rather than on the preacher. Musical words and florid phrases may please listeners, but what profit do these provide? Homilies like this are often entertainment, nothing more. Unless listeners can easily follow the preacher, they will readily give up or doze off; they might even become apathetic, bored, resentful, and even hostile.

Undoubtedly, one of the enemies of simplicity is ambiguity. This occurs when a phrase is overloaded with qualifications, or when two negatives clash. For example, "I would not hesitate to say that the present spirit of enterprise is not likely to abate." Compound sentences are not used frequently in popular conversation and should therefore be used sparingly in preaching. They often exhaust the listener, much like one can be tired by reading Cicero and some of Karl Rahner's writings.

Short sentences are extremely effective when speaking outdoors or in a large auditorium. Martin Luther King, Jr., did this well when he proclaimed "I have a dream." Short sentences are generally clearer than long, involved sentences. On the other hand, a preponderance of them can sound staccato and stilted. Longer sentences often help the preacher unfold one's thought, but too many of these tire the listener or enmesh the audience in a word trap. The ideal is to have a combination of long and short sentences, with a preference for the short sentence.

I once made a study of the average length of sentences in homilies of certain well known preachers and public speakers. I found that, overall, the average length is about twenty-one words per sentence. Here are some specifics: for Fulton Sheen, it was twenty-five; for Cyprian Truss, twenty-two; for Joseph Manton, twenty-one; for Walter Burghardt, fifteen. See how this compares with other speakers known for their simple style: Franklin Roosevelt, whose average was twenty-three words per sentence; Wendell Phillips, twenty-three; and Winston Churchill, twenty-six. It is evident that the above-mentioned preachers compare favorably to speakers who were known for their simple style.

Short sentences add clarity to a homily because the ideas can more readily be grasped and understood. Yet a preacher should not make false simplifications for the sake of being understood. Balance is the key to making the message both intelligible and rhythmical.

When we adopt simple language, simple thinking, simple and familiar words, and simple sentences, we will begin to use the language of Jesus. His language was simple, straightforward, and clear. Jesus employed an economy of words in his Sermon on the Mount, which has been described as a model of sublime coherency. We are invited to imitate the master.

9 ILLUSTRATIONS

"Therefore, to keep me from being too elated, a thorn was given me in the flesh…" (2 Cor 12:7). A parishioner, who was listening to a homily on this passage from Paul, was not very impressed until the end, when the preacher offered this illustration: A man played a record twice for his friend, then asked: "Which did you prefer?" The friend responded, "The second; it was purer and sweeter." His host informed him: "The first was played with a needle. The second with a thorn."

The power of illustrations to enliven homilies cannot be overestimated. Illustrations can add clarity to an abstract idea, or elaborate on a profound thought. Often hearers respond to preaching by thinking, "We've heard all that before." A good illustration can counteract that reaction. Well chosen illustrations often banish dullness and boredom from the pulpit.

Homilies with illustrations are more easily remembered. People will often recall a story or anecdote and then be able to more readily remember the point of the homily. Here is an example. In her book, *A Slender Thread,* Diane Ackerman tells the story of Jack Lewis, an eighty-year-old Protestant minister. He received a wrenching phone call one morning from a man who was holding a gun on his wife and children. Jack Lewis was courageous enough to walk into his home, sit down next to the man and say, "Tell me your story." After ten hours the man gave Jack his gun. Ackerman went on to show that many of us have a "loaded gun" in our lives. But once we have told our story, we might be ready to lay it down.

Illustrative preaching can be most persuasive. An emotional story can have a deep impact and move hearers to action, such as this: A Russian woman's son was court martialed and executed on the eve of World War II. The grieving mother searched out the soldier who had fired the shot that killed her son, only to discover that the man was critically ill and near death. The mother nursed him back to life—and then adopted him.

Illustrations help to alleviate repetition from a homily by allowing a preacher to approach the topic from a different angle. You could try a story like this to add a different twist to a homily on the Scripture passage about Zacchaeus (Lk 19:2–10): Oliver Wendell Holmes once attended a meeting, and happened to be the smallest person present. "Dr. Holmes," quipped a friend, "I should think you'd feel rather small among us big fellows." "I do," retorted Holmes, "I feel like a dime among a lot of pennies."

Types of illustrations

It is often said that variety is the spice of life, and there are no truer words than this when applied to illustrations. Variety adds freshness and vitality to preaching. Figures of speech are one forceful way to get a point across. Here are some examples:

Metaphors

Scripture scholar John Dominic Crossan makes a distinction between metaphors of illustration and metaphors of participation. Metaphors of illustration are stories that explain the point a preacher is trying to make. If we are preaching about the sinister nature of sin, we might use an illustration such as the story of Adam and Eve to drive home the point. Thus we can show that the basic temptation to sin has remained down through the ages; we all have an innate desire to "be like God, knowing good and evil"(Gen 3:5).

Metaphors of participation are even more effective because the hearers participate in the story. The reality of the text becomes the reality of the hearer. A powerful metaphor for human sin can be found in Colleen McCullough's book, *Thorn Birds*: "The bird with the thorn in the breast, it follows an immutable law; it is driven by it knows not what to impale itself, and dies singing. At the very instant the thorn enters there is no awareness in it of the dying to come; it simply sings and sings until there is not the life left to utter another note. But, we, when we put the thorns in our breast, we know. We understand. And still we do it. Still we do it."

Metaphors enhance the meaning of our words. They are implied comparisons. Look at the beauty within the phrases "You are the light of the world" or "You are the salt of the earth."

Parables

A parable is a developed simile, while allegories, like William Golding's *Lord of the Flies,* or C.S. Lewis's *Chronicles of Narnia,* are developed metaphors. Jesus told parables not only to stimulate his hearers but also to allow them to draw their own conclusions. Jesus told the crowds all these things in parables; without a parable he told them nothing. This was to fulfill what had been spoken through the prophet: "I will open my mouth to speak in parables; I will proclaim what has been hidden from the foundation of the world" (Mt 13:34–35).

The parable of the prodigal son is an invitation for listeners to come to their senses. It speaks to all people, including you and me, who object when people reach out to AIDS victims; or who glare at crying babies in church; or who won't welcome black or Hispanic people into their community or neighborhood. The story of the prodigal son asks the question: when are we going to break away from our prejudices and hatred and return to the love of our Father?

A modern parable to show how God takes care of us might be the story of a mother eagle and her eaglets. Once the mother decides that her young are ready to fly she puts them on her wings and flies off from the nest. When she reaches a certain height, she collapses her wings and the eaglets start fluttering. Some might begin to fly while others might fall. The mother eagle flies under the struggling ones and catches them. Then she flies higher and the training continues.

Analogies

An analogy focuses on similarities between one situation and another. For example, a preacher was trying to make a point about how people tend to hang on to certain things or ideas. To illustrate this point, he used the analogy of how monkeys are captured. A small, necked jar is half-filled with beans and placed on the ground. More beans are scattered around the jar to attract the monkeys. When the monkeys come near to the jar, they reach in and grab a handful of beans. But once they have made a fist, it is impossible for them to get their hands out. As long as they hold on to the beans, they are stuck. And so all the trapper does next is carry them off.

This analogy shows the need to season a homily so it can become a true verbal feast. Any good chef, like Emeril or Julia Child, doesn't use exact measurements for cooking food. He or she often uses the words "about" or "approximately." Likewise, a good preacher needs to learn how to properly season the homily. The ingredients might be a story or illustration, some exegesis, or some pressing issue of importance to the assembly. The ingredients—as well as how much and how little of each element is used—will vary with each preacher.

Sources for illustrations

• The Bible is filled with stories that can be used to exemplify a point. Characters fill the pages of Scripture with marvelous illustrations to focus our preaching. Consider these examples: the heroism of Susanna, Ruth, Esther, Judith, and the mother of the Maccabees; the struggles of Job, Jonah, and Jeremiah; the faithfulness of David and Saul; the responsiveness of Samuel, Matthew, and John; and the repentance of Peter and Dismas, the good thief. These stories lift up the hearts and minds of the congregation, and help Scripture come alive for our listeners.

• Being attentive to nature and marveling at its wonders can also help our preaching. One day, a man was watching a butterfly trying desperately to escape its cocoon. He felt sorry for the butterfly and helped it escape. To his chagrin, the butterfly was unable to fly, and struggled to become airborne. After beating its wings desperately for a few minutes, however, the butterfly soared off into the air. The strenuous attempt to fly strengthened the butterfly's wings and enabled it to soar into the air.

• Theologian Karl Barth insisted that all good preachers must have the Bible in one hand and the newspaper in the other. *Fulfilled in Your Hearing* states: "Preachers need to devote some time and energy to understanding the complex social, political, and economic forces that are shaping the contemporary world. Watching the evening news on television or scanning the headlines of the daily paper may be a beginning, but it is not enough. Preachers need exposure to more serious and sustained commentary on the contemporary world" (#34).

Listeners will be more attentive if we sometimes use examples from current news and events. This technique often enables the preacher to illustrate an idea in a timely and forceful way. A good preacher knows what events are on the minds of the assembly, as well as what events are worth addressing.

• Our choice of reading material will be reflected in our preaching. Hours spent praying over Scripture, delving into church history, or perusing newspapers and magazines, is not wasted time. Reading biographies and fiction can also be most helpful.

I once came across this story in an anthology, which I was then able to incorporate into a homily on social justice: There was a priest in Africa, one of many who took a strong stand against apartheid. Naturally, he created many enemies. One day he received a letter, but was unaware that it was a letter bomb. In the process of opening it, he lost both of his hands and was struck blind. Afterwards, the priest responded to the incident in this way: "They might be able to take my two hands and take away my eyesight, but I will continue to speak out against the injustices of apartheid."

• Most people are intrigued by the experiences of others, because it is often something which they themselves can relate to. Here is an interesting account from Megan McKenna:

A few years ago, traveling in Wales, I did a parish mission in a dark, grim, and poor small town, made nearly all of slate mined in the hills above the town. At night we would sit in a cozy house by a fire, drinking a bit of whiskey and watching the sky darkening and the shadows coming on. It was fascinating.

The house was high in the hills above the town. First there would be one light. Then the minutes would pass and another light, then another. A trail of light wound its way below us, around and in and out. I watched, wondering what it was and how it was created.

My host smiled and said, "Ah, you've noticed. We are still poor and a bit backward here. That is the lamplighter, walking through the town, lighting the gas lamps." Then he said, "There is a saying by John Ruskin that I always recall when I catch sight of the lamps being lit down below in the town: 'You always know you are in a presence of a Christian by the trail of light they leave behind.'"

I remember when my dad was dying in the hospital. I thought that, as a priest, I would be able to help him in a special way. Yet I had never felt so powerless in all my life as when I walked into his room, sat down near his bed, and saw him lying there, frail and ill. My dad looked at me and I looked at him; we did not say much. But our silence spoke volumes. At this point the words of Paul took on a deeper significance for me: "My grace is sufficient for you, for power is made perfect in weakness" (2 Cor 12:9–10).

• Movies can be a forceful way to drive home a point. In *Dead Man Walking,* the murderer finally breaks down and tells the truth about his crimes, making the point that all killing is evil. He is afraid now, and asks Sr. Helen Prejean to comfort him as he is about to die. In a voice cracking with emotion, she bravely tries to sing the hymn "Be Not Afraid." She then tells him, "Look at my face and see the face of Christ. Let the face of Christ be the face you see as you die."

One preacher used the following story from the movie *Titanic* to stress a point about values: A certain woman, who had been allotted a place in one of the lifeboats, asked if she might run back to her stateroom. She was given three minutes to do so. The woman hurried along the corridors, already tilting at a dangerous angle, and crossed the saloon. Money and costly gems littered the floor, as some of the people who had snatched up their valuables had dropped them as they ran. In her own stateroom were many treasures waiting to be picked up. She saw them, but took no heed. Snatching at three oranges which she knew to be there as well, she ran back to take her place in the lifeboat.

• Other sources—such as painting, music, architecture, sculpture, plays, novels, popular songs, and travel—can also offer inspiration and examples to illustrate our preaching. Some might object, however, that preaching that uses illustration lacks depth. But great thinkers, like philosopher Immanuel Kant, used illustration to clarify their most profound thoughts. So did Jesus.

As I mentioned at the start of this chapter, illustrations clarify abstract ideas. They counteract a ho-hum response, and banish thoughts like, "Here we go again; another boring homily." Illustrations add freshness or a new angle to a homily. So get busy— and start illustrating!

10 STORYTELLING

"Storytelling is as natural as breathing–as old as the stone age and as current as Garrison Keillor," wrote Murray Elwood. And Anthony de Mello once said, "The shortest distance between a human being and truth is a story."

Most people love a story—children certainly do. Anyone who has spent time with children knows they can hear the same stories over and over again and never tire of them. There is a fascination about storytelling that defies description. Stories get listener's attention. An assembly might not remember much about our homily, but they will not forget a story well told.

Meaningful stories definitely enhance our homilies. They are a way to create and construct meaning, a way to help listeners step into our stream of thought. Stories engage people in relationships, and are a fundamental way to perceive reality. They help us to look upon ancient landscapes with a fresh eye. Jesus was a master storyteller because he possessed a keen sense of observation. He was able to incorporate a story into a particular truth he was trying to get across. John Shea is a modern-day preacher who is very good at writing and telling stories. Many of his stories are gems, and you don't need a jeweler's eyepiece to understand the message. He insists that stories be preachable, personable, and have pastoral meaning.

Stories have many advantages. They provoke curiosity and bind us to all of humankind, to the universal, human family. They are a bridge to our culture, our roots. Stories unite us holistically to all of nature. They help us to remember, and they evoke our imaginations. Stories use a special language and restore the original power of the word, allowing for a multiplicity of meaning. They are readily remembered, and so can emphasize the point of a homily.

This story gives a humorous angle to the gospel passage from Luke, where Jesus rebukes the lawyers (11:45–48): Ulysses S. Grant was known to dress very shabbily. One day, while traveling, he came to an inn in Galena, Illinois, where a group of lawyers had gathered around a fire. One of the lawyers said to Grant, "Here's a stranger, gentlemen, and by the looks of him he's traveled through hell itself to get here." "That's right," Grant responded with a cheerful smile. "And how did you find things down there?" the attorney persisted. "Just like here," replied Grant. "The lawyers were all closest to the fire."

In his book, *Media: The Second God,* Anthony Schwarz maintains that we have become a post-literate society. "Electronic media, rather than the printed word, are now our major means of non-face-to-face communication." Because of this, stories are a natural part of preaching in the post-literate age. Many—if not most—people spend a great deal of time wired into various forms of electronic communication. In much of this media, it is the ear that is primarily engaged. Some communication experts have called our age "secondarily oral"; the ears have made a comeback in our culture.

An oral vs. literate culture

In what ways does a primarily oral culture differ from a literate culture? Richard Jensen, a Lutheran homiletics professor, makes the following distinctions. The oral culture appeals to the ear, while the literate, to the eye. Oral culture stitches stories together; the literate develops ideas in a linear fashion. Oral culture often uses repetition, like "down with dope and up with hope"; the literate culture deals more with structured ideas.

Oral culture uses situational experiences while the literate proposes main points. The oral often utilizes conflict; the literate is more analytical. The oral appeals to the right brain, while the literate relies on the left brain and is more logical. The oral uses metaphors of participation, the literate, metaphors of illustration. The goal of oral culture is participation, whereas the goal of the literate culture is understanding. And so, in consideration of all these factors, if we are to preach in an oral culture a paradigm shift might be necessary in our thinking.

How did people communicate in previous oral cultures? They did so primarily by narrating stories. To effectively communicate today, preachers need to recapture the skill of storytelling. In his book, *Jesus for a New Generation,* Kevin Graham Ford states:

> The concept of story or narrative gives us a new way of looking at evangelism and a new paradigm for reaching my genera-tion....This approach to evangelism is ideally suited for reaching the soul of Generation X because it is a "new-old" approach. It is a new approach when compared to other twentieth-century strategies because it has not been actively attempted until recent-ly. It is an old approach because it is the same approach used by Jesus himself and by the early evangelists.

When people are attuned to electronic forms of communication (e.g., telephones, radio, television, the Internet), they often come to liturgy with the expectation of a sensory experience. Those who read throughout the week are more satisfied with a liturgy that is literate or informational. A good preacher needs to be aware that the homi-ly must be addressed to both experiences, on one level or another.

In *God of the Oppressed,* James H. Cone asks, "What then is the form and content of black religious thought when viewed in the light of their social situation? Briefly, the form of black religious thought is expressed in the style of story and its content is liberation....White theologians built logical systems; black folks told tales."

When preachers explain Christian truth they often demand an understanding from their listeners. When we tell stories we are trying to evoke Christian reality and invite deeper participation. Forgiveness, for example, becomes no longer just a doctrine to be understood. Rather, it is an experience that captures our imagination and brings us to tears or to joy.

A good story will make listeners resonate with what is being told. As Megan McKenna, herself a master storyteller, writes: "One of the reasons we laugh at stories is because they are about us, and our laughter says that we acknowledge they are really about us."

Can you relate to this story? A child was fishing with his grandfather, but the fish were not biting that day. "Be patient," said the grandfather to the boy. The child responded, "How long do I have to be patient?"

Stories like these become a mirror which preachers hold up to themselves and their listeners. We are known by the stories we tell; we become what we narrate.

Know your story

Most stories need to be told without an explanation. If it is a strong story and well told, revelation happens as the assembly listens to the story. If the story has the elements you need to make your point, leave it alone. And don't be afraid to pause; the richest and deepest part of a story is often found in the silences between the words, or at the end of the story. Above all, don't cultivate the intellectual understanding of a story; that simply fosters a head trip.

Be aware that there are two sides to a story, the inner and outer, the warp and the woof. We listen with our inner ear to the inner story. We accent the outer story by how we act, dress, and come across to others. If our whole life is an outside story, we may not be in contact with our feelings. Likewise, if we are too directed inward, we may lose touch with our listeners. A good example of the balance between an inner and outer story is found in the *Confessions* of Augustine.

Many stories, particularly those in the gospels, are well known. And so Paul Ricoeur recommends that we change the titles of stories as one way to give them a new twist. Instead of telling the story of the prodigal son, we can call it the story of the prodigal father. We can develop this perspective by asking further questions about the prodigal father story: Were the hired workers (or were they slaves?) recipients of the father's liberality? Were they involved in the celebration? (It is telling that in the story, when the younger son repents of his wanton ways, he considers the status of the hired workers, and how they are better off than he at this point.) A discussion of how the father responds to the hired workers might provoke a reflection on certain groups of workers who are often taken for granted and yet perform vital ministries–like custodians or secretaries, to name two.

We can take another direction with this story, asking our listeners questions such as these: Did you notice how the father runs to his son once he spots him at a distance? In the Arab world, a man would never run because of his long robes or the danger of showing his legs. Then, against custom, it was the son who spoke first when he met his father. And what the son said—"Father, I have sinned against heaven and before you; I am no longer worthy to be called your son"— was shocking! It was not a legitimate request for a son to make of his father. And did you notice how the father does not explode, but gives his son ultimate freedom? Good preachers jerk the assembly out of their complacency when telling stories that are well known.

Stories from the Bible

Thomas Boomershine's book, *Story Journey: An Invitation to the Gospel as Storytelling,* points out and emphasizes the reasons for biblical storytelling. (The book also offers practical advice on how to master this art.) Many stories in the Bible were stitched together to communicate the author's message. Thus, they invite listeners to participate in their reality.

Bible stories are able to penetrate our cultural defenses and cultivate our imagination. There is tremendous power that can be unleashed by telling the stories of Jonah, Job, Ruth, or Esther. Many preachers have been trained to fill their listeners with ideas–and ideas certainly have their place in preaching. But we also need to fill their hearts with the stories of people. And what better place to find stories about good (and bad) people—people like all of us, in fact— than in the Bible?

Biblical stories should be told in such a way that they come alive in the hearts and minds of our listeners. But they have to come alive in us first. Let's take the Book of Daniel as an example of how an ancient story can be made relevant for our times. The events in the Book of Daniel took place in Babylon during the exile. The book, however, was written hundreds of years after the exile. It spoke to an entirely different culture.

The first six chapters are inspiring stories of how the faith was preserved amidst trying circumstances. Daniel and several other young men were taken to the court of King Nebuchednezzar, where they were to be trained as court slaves. There they were given rich food to eat. But they asked for vegetables instead, that they could grow healthy by God's grace. Preachers can take this point–that is, the overconsumption of rich foods and material wealth–and apply it to United States today. They can show how the United States consumes a disproportionate amount of the world's energy and goods.

When Daniel and his companions were given "vegetables to eat and water to drink," after ten days they "looked healthier and better fed than any of the young men who ate from the royal table" (Dn 1:11–16). Imagine what might happen to our society if many people took that kind of risk: not to eat junk food or food rich in calories. That is another challenge found in this story, which we can offer to our listeners.

Many other accounts that bear fruit for our times can be found in Daniel, like the story of the golden statue in chapter three. Nebuchednezzar ordered all to fall down and worship the statue when they came upon it, or be thrown into a furnace of burning flame. Three of Daniel's companions refused to bow down, and so were thrown into the fire. There, the king saw a man with "the appearance of a god" walking in the furnace with the three (3:92). And so the king recognized the presence of the true God, and ordered the men to come out from the fire, where they were found to be completely unharmed. Thus, we can ask: What are the images of gold which we worship in our culture? Might not the "son of God" accompany us also if we have more trust and courage?

Richard A. Jensen wrote this: "Biblical stories are dynamite. They are powerful in and of themselves. They are powerful without much explanatory help from us. They work. They do what they promise to do. Biblical stories participate in the reality of the grace which they announce."

Jesus was the master storyteller. He used parables and stories from people's daily lives to reach their hearts and minds. Even today, many families have a prodigal son or daughter, a jealous brother or sister. Jesus knew there were people who made promises and did not keep them; widows who shared everything; people clamoring for places of honor; wise and foolish virgins. He told stories relating to commerce: the farmer sowing seed, the harvest, a lost sheep, the coin of tribute, a man killed in a vineyard, fishermen who toiled with their nets, debtors hauled into court. Jesus drew stories from nature: the lilies of the field, the birds of the air, productive and non-productive trees, mustard seed, good soil and bad soil.

How did Jesus learn these stories? He did not have a library of anthologies at his disposal, nor could he look up "stories" on the Internet. No, the stories that Jesus told were developed over time. (Remember that he began his public life at the age of thirty.) Some of the stories he learned from Mary and Joseph, while others he heard at various gatherings, like weddings or funerals. Many he gleaned from his conversations with the temple teachers over the years.

We read in the gospels that Mary "treasured all these things in her heart" (Lk 2:51). Jesus undoubtedly did the same with the stories he heard throughout his life, and pondered them when he went away to pray. We are invited to do the same.

Taking a broader view

When considering the scriptural texts, especially the gospels, a preacher might ask if there are any other stories that help clarify this text or are linked to it. "Panoramic" exegesis can give a much broader view, as other stories shed new light or meaning on a particular text.

Here is an example: There is an evident reversal of roles brought out in Mary's "Magnificat" when she says, "He has brought down the powerful from their thrones, and lifted up the lowly..." (Lk 1:52). This same type of reversal is found when Jesus says, "Indeed, some are last who will be first, and some are first who will be last" (Lk 13:30). These words are echoed in Luke: "For all who exalt themselves will be humbled, and those who humble themselves will be exalted" (14:11). Mary's "Magnificat" can also be compared to Hannah's prayer in 1 Samuel (2:1–10), especially when she says: "He raises up the poor from the dust; he lifts the needy from the ash heap, to make them sit with princes and inherit a seat of honor."

The gospel writers had a wide range of stories to choose from when writing down the Scripture. They selected stories that helped depict the life of Jesus for a particular audience. When we examine the stories in the gospels, we should consider why one story precedes another, or how a certain story fits into the overall framework of the gospel. Preachers need to be careful not to study texts in isolation– "microscopic" exegesis–but see them in a broader context.

Garrison Keillor, an outstanding contemporary storyteller, stated in an interview:

I think people do want to hear the gospel in the form of a story. There's a story at the heart of every sermon. I think sermons fail when they take that story, stick it in a corner, and make it into a lecture. That won't work for people….A story allows people to come into it. You can somehow envision yourself as a participant in a story. It engages the imagination in a way that a lecture does not…a story has a magical power to draw people into it.

Storytelling is an ideal medium for our post-literate culture. The twofold challenge for preachers is to gather meaningful stories, especially biblical stories, and to become a good storyteller. Remember, too, that we write our own gospel story with our experiences, trials, hardships, joys, and happiness. Through time, these stories can be stitched together into a cohesive whole.

Truly, the art of storytelling is one of the powerful ways to communicate a message as we imitate the master storyteller, Jesus. Are you ready for a story?

11 PERSUASION

The word "persuasion" comes from two Latin words, *per* and *suasio,* meaning "through sweetness." Interesting, isn't it? It brings to mind the expression, "You can catch more flies with honey...." Persuasion is an attempt to move hearers to an opinion or conviction. It connotes the power to change attitudes, arouse emotions, and stimulate action.

Aristotle defined rhetoric as "the faculty of discovering in every case the available means of persuasion." (Not everyone agrees about his use of the qualifier "every case.") He also considered *ethos,* or the characteristics of a speaker, the most important facet in persuasion. This is exemplified by what was said of one beloved pastor: "He could stand up and read his laundry list, and we would be moved to tears." Right or wrong, listeners often respond more to the preacher than to the homily itself.

When a preacher fails to "practice what is preached," it is hard for that person to give a persuasive homily. And so, it might be difficult for an obese preacher who proclaims the need to fast and mortify oneself to be taken seriously by the assembly. If the hearers know the preacher's lifestyle is rather extravagant, that preacher's plea for a simpler lifestyle will fall on deaf ears. When little action is taken by a preacher in the area of social justice or ecology, few hearers, if any, will be moved to change their point of view regarding these areas of concern.

Yet the opposite is also true. The reason Jesus was effective in his preaching was that he practiced what he preached. Mother Teresa of Calcutta's success can be traced to the fact that she saw Jesus Christ in the person of the poor and sick—and lived based on that vision. Dom Helder Camara was well known for his courageous crusade against injustice and oppression in Central America. He spoke out against the torture and murder of political dissidents, and, like Jesus, suffered much persecution because of this.

Kenneth Burke maintains that a good preacher "woos the audience." We can compare ourselves to the lover wooing the beloved as depicted in the Song of Songs. This does not mean that we must be syrupy or sickeningly sentimental. It does mean engaging the hearers with a desire to change their behavior or attitude.

The prophet Nathan did this well when he confronted David about the death of Uriah (2 Sam 12:1-13). As you may recall, David had Uriah killed in battle so that he could have Bathsheba. Nathan set a trap for David by telling him a story about a rich man who stole a poor man's ewe. By using this analogy, Nathan forced David to come to his own conclusion about his wrongdoing in the death of Uriah. Likewise, good preachers hold a mirror up to their hearers so they can see their true selves, the way Nathan did to David.

Passion needed

Passion makes a preacher more persuasive. It took passion to inscribe the words written by the authors of Scripture, and it takes passion to lift them off the page. Passion is generated by something real, like loneliness, the loss of a loved one, or some other universal experience. Jesus said, "I came to bring fire to the earth, and how I wish it were already kindled!" (Lk 12:49). Yet he kindled that fire in the hearts of the people by his persuasive messages.

Passionate preaching is as contagious as yawning, tears, or joy; it makes the assembly want to listen. God's word has to get under our skin and become like a song we keep humming over and over. Jonah spent three days in the belly of the whale before he was ready to preach passionately to the Ninevites: "Forty days and Nineveh shall be destroyed" (Jon 3:4-9). Then they repented—even the king.

Paul must have been a most dynamic preacher because of the way he could persuade people to turn their lives over to Christ. No wonder he could exhort the people: "In the presence of God and of Christ Jesus, who is to judge the living and the dead, and in view of his appearing and his kingdom, I solemnly urge you: proclaim the message; be persistent whether the time is favorable or unfavorable; convince, rebuke, and encourage, with the utmost patience in teaching" (2 Tim 4:1–2).

The most memorable teachers are often those most moved by their own lectures. Isn't this true of memorable preachers? Some of the teachers and preachers who have really stood out for me are those who delivered their lectures or homilies in a passionate way.

Martin Luther King, Jr., spoke with much passion, especially about the possibility of a violent death. He told his followers during a Selma march: "I can't promise you that it won't get you beaten. I can't promise you that it won't get your home bombed. I can't promise you won't get scared up a bit; but we must stand up for what is right. If you haven't discovered something that is worth dying for, you haven't found anything worth living for." King certainly did.

At times, preachers need to use what theorists call "counter-attitudinal" messages. That means stating the opposite of what you believe, for example, telling the assembly that we need to hate our enemies. This type of statement will usually arouse the listeners attention, and then the preacher can explain how this is contrary to Jesus' message. How often have we tried to persuade people to love their enemies? We know much about love, but do we challenge our listeners to practice the highest kind of love, that is, love of our enemies?

Stories are another way to persuade, especially those that grip the hearers and are well told. They invite participation, and usually imply some movement will follow. Stories have a magnetic effect on hearers because they combine action, dialogue, and emotion. As the popular preacher Fred Craddock states, they touch "all the keys on the board rather than only the intellectual, or emotional, or volitional." Stories such as those found in *Aesop's Fables* demonstrate how persuasion has always been deemed better than force.

If we are trying to persuade our hearers not to be heartbroken because of some failure, we might tell the following story found in the *Chicken Soup for the Soul* series:

A husband came home discouraged because he lost his job. But his wife, Sophia, simply said to him, "Now you can write your book."

"But what are we going to live on," he replied.

She opened a drawer and showed him a large amount of money, explaining that she had saved this because she was convinced he was a genius and could write. This man did write a book, *The Scarlet Letter,* and we know his name: Nathaniel Hawthorne.

Humor is an effective means of making hearers more receptive to your message. It is a gentle way to disarm the hearers and make them more responsive to God's word. Here's a humorous story about the importance of always telling the truth. A certain teacher told a group of second graders the story of Ananias and Sapphira, who dropped dead when they lied to Peter. After the story, one little child raised his hand and said, "If God did that today, there would not be many people left." You might follow up this story by asking: "Has anyone here never told a lie? If so, then please stand." Then you can comment, "See, no one is standing (pause), except me—and that is a lie!"

Involvement

Persuasive preachers are challenged to involve the hearers by making them participants: If this is the situation, what do we do now? The aim here is to challenge the assembly to make a decision.

Persuasive preaching is often crisis oriented: We encounter God in a particular situation, and must answer yes or no to the call. Too many preachers allow a neutral response rather than provoke the assembly. Sometimes this is due to the fear of a negative response. Yet we must learn to accept a "no" from our hearers; remember, not everyone responded to Jesus' invitation to follow him. We have to realize there may often be opposition to our message. A group of people in a parish or community are seldom of one mind on any given matter, and so we have to bridge the chasm.

One preacher challenged his congregation by asking: "Are we 'saints' or 'ain'ts,' saints in church, but ain'ts in the world?" Many people have formed certain attitudes toward life that are not easily changed. As Walter Burghardt states: "Too many of us despise red folk and black, yellow and brown, all too many still consider the Jewish people 'Christ killers.' In fact, rather than say 'all too many of us,' I must look with utter honesty into my own heart, must ask how often, like the priest and Levite in Luke, I too have 'passed by on the other side' (Lk 10:31–32)."

Persuasive preachers need to be welcome intruders into the hearts and minds of the assembly, to help change these attitudes. It does no good to rant and rave about all the evils in the world without challenging people to find a solution. Some preachers use the hypodermic-needle approach, thinking that hearers can be persuaded against their wills. Yet this seldom is effective. Persuasive preaching disturbs the hearers, not just edifies. Anthony de Mello was aware of his powers of persuasion, and often warned others: "Don't let yourselves be hypnotized by me."

Some preachers think that more is better when trying to persuade. But what is left unsaid is just as important, or more so, than what was said. A good poet uses an economy of words. Ezra Pound maintains that we ought to "crowd maximum meaning into the single phrase, pregnant, charged, and luminous from within."

You may be familiar with the expression *multum in parvum* (much in little). In this regard, consider the brevity of many advertising slogans, and how they have become part of our everyday language, like, "Think different," "Where's the beef?" and "Just do it." Persuasive preachers too need something catchy, like: Are you in a rut? Then make the proposal: Do you want to get out of the rut? Answer the need: This is the way you get out. Give the proof, whatever is appropriate. Finally, issue a call for action!

Jesus stirred his hearers to anger when he told the parable of the laborers who killed the heir of the vineyard. But his audience failed to condemn themselves. David was angered by the story of the ewe told him by the prophet Nathan, but he failed to make the connection between his own actions and the rich man's until Nathan pointed it out. Likewise, we must experience the emotions that we want to express.

Paul stirred up many emotions in his preaching, with the intention to convert his audience. He wrote: "We also constantly give thanks to God for this, that when you received the word of God that you heard from us, you accepted it not as a human word but as what it really is, God's word, which is also at work in you believers" (1 Thess 2:13). He almost persuaded King Agrippa, who said, "Are you so quickly persuading me to become a Christian?" (Acts 26:28).

Commenting on this passage, Frederick Buechner states: "If only Paul had been a little more eloquent. If only Agrippa had been a little more receptive, a little braver, a little crazier. If only God weren't such a stickler for letting people make up their own minds without coercing them." Preachers will say "Amen" to that.

Self-persuasion

Robin Meyers, in his book *With Ears to Hear,* describes self-persuasion as "what happens when a message gets people talking to themselves." It suggests that persuasion is ultimately a self-generated rather than other-generated phenomenon, the object of which is to elicit a kind of intrapersonal conversation in the listener. A good example can be found in the play *Fiddler on the Roof,* when Tevye argues with God and waits for the answers to life's mysteries. By listening to himself and to his questions, the answers come.

If the listeners must be involved in the homily in order for it to be effective, the preacher must do the same. The question the preacher asks may no longer be "Are you listening to me?" but "Does listening to me get you talking to yourself?" In self-persuasion, the preacher does not want the last word but wants to give listeners an opportunity to respond "yes" or "no." As James wrote in his epistle: "But be doers of the word, and not merely hearers who deceive themselves" (1:22). The preacher should be the first one to be persuaded by a homily. A good preacher casts a spell on oneself before doing so on others.

Preachers have to be convinced of what they are preaching, otherwise we become what Paul calls "a noisy gong or a clanging cymbal." According to Gerard Sloyan, preachers can become dancing bears, mindlessly performing their routines.

John Courtney Murray, SJ, once stated: "I do not know what I have said until I understand what you have heard." In final analysis, the persuasive preacher is only a word that is heard, always aware that God speaks through the preacher. We might stutter like Jeremiah did, or need cleansing of our lips as Isaiah did, or seek the courage of Amos or John the Baptist's fearlessness. Yet we can all depend on God's grace to touch people's hearts.

As Augustine states, "God himself is the persuader in good preaching."

12   HUMOR

We have touched on the use of humor in preaching in previous chapters. Now I would like to look at this topic in a bit more depth.

Some preachers don't approve of humor in a homily, and question if it is appropriate to laugh in church. Maybe the real question here is: Does God have a sense of humor? As one comedian replied: "He certainly does, because he created me." Although I respect people and preachers who don't approve of it, I want to show that humor, if used appropriately, does have a place in preaching.

The story of Balaam's talking donkey is evidence of God's sense of humor, as well as of the lengths God will go to to get across a message. (If you are not familiar with this story, give yourself a treat and read it in Numbers 22:1–35.) And the story of the dry bones found in Ezekiel (37:1–14) is a humorous reminder of how weary we can become at times. Is it a coincidence that the word "joy" appears over 200 times in Scripture?

Jesus is often depicted as a man of sorrows, but he was also a man of tremendous joy. He displayed a wide range of human emotions, and revealed the joy of living in God's love. Vincent Giese maintains, "If Jesus was the most balanced of persons, he certainly must have possessed a certain quality of joy and a keen sense of humor, and have been able to laugh."

Many Scripture scholars have shown how Jesus possessed a sense of humor in preaching. The eight Beatitudes, which can be called the Magna Carta of Christianity, portray him as a person who knew what it meant to rejoice. (Note that Jesus never said, "Blessed are the melancholy.") His joyful spirit was manifested at the wedding in

Cana when he changed water into wine. (Or, as the English poet Richard Crashaw put it, the water saw its God and blushed.)

I can't imagine that Jesus did not have a good belly laugh when he saw Zacchaeus perched up in a sycamore tree, or when the men cleverly lowered the paralytic down through the roof in front of him. He enjoyed children, and wanted them to come to him. He knew that the apostles were in anguish at the last supper when he said, "I will see you again, and your hearts will rejoice, and no one will take your joy from you" (Jn 16:22).

Jesus wished that his apostles could share his joy completely. "But now I am coming to you, and I speak these things in the world so that they may have my joy made complete in themselves" (Jn 17:13). Picture the interplay between Jesus and the disciples on the road to Emmaus when they asked him, "Are you the only stranger in Jerusalem who does not know the things that have taken place there in these days?" And Jesus rather slyly replied, "What things?" (Lk 24:18–19). It is too bad that none of the evangelists wrote "Jesus began to laugh," which could be contrasted with "Jesus began to weep."

Pope Paul VI wrote a papal document on the gift of joy, *Gaudete in Domino*. In it he maintained that joy is one of the characteristics of any saint, and used the example of Maximilian Kolbe as an example of someone who transformed the hell of Auschwitz into an antechamber to eternal life. Paul VI stressed the need for joy in the contemporary world, and encouraged Christians to share their joy with others. In a later document on evangelization, he exhorted Christians that to effectively evangelize one must proclaim the good news with joy.

It is important for preachers to point out that joy and sorrow can exist alongside the other. The poet Kahlil Gibran insisted that joy is sorrow unmasked, and that laughter is often mixed with tears. As Paul proclaimed God's power made perfect in weakness, we too can proclaim Jesus' joy made perfect in sorrow.

The quality of joy is certainly most appreciated in times of adversity or hardship. Albert Schweitzer found joy while ministering in Africa to people plagued with sores. Despite being in prison and suffering many hardships, Paul could write one of the most joy-filled letters to the Philippians: "Christ is proclaimed in every way, whether out of false motives or true; and in that I rejoice. Yes, and I will continue to rejoice…" (1:18). What consoling words for any proclaimer of good news!

The fact that Paul could thrive under stressful circumstances points out the difference between happiness and joy. For most First World people, happiness depends on the amount of material goods they possess, or on whether life is going their way. Joy transcends material means, and can exist even when deprivation is present.

Preachers need to be anointed with joy. We should muse over the joy of being alive, the joy of friendships, the joy of ministering to others, the joy of leisure time (the Greeks believed it was only through leisure that we could be joyful), and the joy of our vocation. True joy, however, can never be appreciated until we share it with others.

Camus wrote that the vocation of artists is "to give a voice to the sorrows and joys of all." Every good preacher is like an artist, proclaiming the good news that Jesus has died for our sins and is truly risen from the dead. The joy of Christ's resurrection is a gift that challenges us to be alleluia preachers. In Greece, it is the custom to observe Easter Monday as a day of laughter to celebrate the joke God played on Satan by raising Jesus from the dead. Truly, the resurrection is God's last laugh on the devil.

Laughing out loud

In Eugene O'Neill's play, *Lazarus Laughed,* there is this constant refrain:

Laugh with me!
Death is dead!
Fear is no more!
There is only life!
There is only laughter!

During this play, the audience hears Lazarus's infectious laugh and begins laughing also.

Laughter can be another name for wisdom because laughter helps us keep things in perspective. It is a gift from the God who is not only a God of surprises, but also a God of laughter. (I once read that Martin Luther stated he did not want to go to heaven if God would not laugh at a joke.)

Laughter can heal hurts and reconcile broken relationships. It is comparable to the balm of Gilead, or to the healing Jesus applied to the sick and outcast. "Laughter is the miracle drug you carry with you all day long that costs nothing," says George Lewis. Laughter can lighten our burdens and give us a lift when we need one. It makes us more human, as well as opens us more to God's graces.

According to some statistics, women laugh twice as much as men— even if they don't get the point of the humor. It is amazing to note that children laugh 300 times each day. Laughter can be far more beneficial than aerobic exercise, and it definitely reduces stress and tension.

Philip Neri had two favorite books: a Bible and a joke book. And who can forget the classic story about the early Church martyr, Lawrence? It is said that when he was being burned on the gridiron, he asked to be turned over, saying "I'm done on this side." (Because of this, Lawrence is one of the patron saints of cooks!) When we consider all the people who have ever lived, why is it no one has ever died of laughter?

There is a group called the Fellowship of Merry Christians (P.O. Box 660, Kalamazoo, MI 49005–0668), whose aim is to recapture the spirit of joy, humor and unity of the early Church. The group has several publications, including a picture called "The Laughing Jesus." There are other books available that contain jokes for use in church, most notably by Monsignor Arthur Tonne and by Tal D. Bonham. (You can find more information on these in the resource list in the back of this book.)

A few years back, the *Detroit News* reprinted a picture by Jack Jewell called "The Risen Christ by the Sea." They then asked readers to respond to this question: Do you think Jesus should be portrayed smiling? Eight out of ten people who answered said yes. When asked to draw a picture of Jesus, children will most often portray him as smiling. The parables of Jesus can be seen as "jokes" where God does the impossible with impossible people.

In *The Divine Comedy,* in the twenty-ninth canto of "Paradiso," Beatrice tells Dante about preachers: "Christ did not say to his first company: 'Go forth and preach garbage unto the world,' but gave them, rather, truth to build upon." She was addressing this comment to preachers she did not like. But she is not finished: "Now men go forth to preach wisecracks and jokes, and just as long as they can get a laugh to puff their cowls with pride–that's all they want." This caution against using humor merely for the purpose of getting a laugh–rather than to emphasize a point–can well be heeded by preachers today.

People don't want jokesters, preachers who can't give a homily without telling a joke. For these people, the preaching event has to begin or end with a joke, or have one sandwiched in somewhere. They sometimes mistake themselves for stand-up comedians. Preachers need to make sure their humor fits the particular point they are trying to get across. If it is to preach the gospel with authority and power, while using humor to get a point across, this is certainly a wiser approach.

Humor is a serious thing

Aristotle made it very clear there was a close relationship between wit and intelligence. Thomas Aquinas is said to have baptized Aristotle's wit. (Wasn't it Thomas who recommended that those who were sad take a bath?) And Hilaire Belloc wrote:

Where'er the Catholic sun doth shine
There is laughter and music and good red wine
At least I always found it so,
Benedicamus Domino.

A good example of someone who combined humor and eloquence was Monsignor Kenneth Velo, the head of the Catholic Church Extension Society. Velo was a friend of the late Joseph Cardinal Bernardin, and preached the eulogy at his funeral. He was able to mimic the Cardinal and tell humorous incidents about the events and places they visited, profoundly moving the assembled mourners.

Humor can often make an audience more attentive to the message—and that's better than having them stare at the cobwebs on the church ceiling or spend their time coughing and shuffling around. Preachers who weave humor into their preaching, making it an integral part of their homily, will arouse and keep the audience's interest.

In one of the many *Peanuts* cartoons from the talented pen of Charles Schultz, Linus is telling Charlie Brown: "When I grow up, I'd like to study about people." Charlie has a puzzled look about him. Linus continues: "People interest me...I'd like to go to some big university and study all about people." Charlie responds: "I see...you want to learn about people so that with your knowledge you will be equipped to help people." Linus replies, "No, I'm just nosy."

Because humor is part and parcel of real life, it can make preaching more relevant. "Preachers see the funny side of people," said the late Minnie Pearl. That doesn't mean we have to be a Will Rogers or a Garrison Keillor, well known humorists who have lifted the spirits of thousands of people with their words. But it does mean that preachers should develop and use a good sense of humor to help take the sting out of the harsh realities of life.

The gospel should be preached so that it brings a smile instead of a frown, a laugh instead of sadness, love instead of hate, hope instead of despair, faith instead of doubt, and light instead of darkness. As someone has said, there should be a ninth beatitude: "Blessed are they who laugh at themselves, for they will never cease to be amused." Proud people cannot laugh at themselves.

In many Native American tribes, four skills are needed to be an official storyteller: a desire to learn the history of the tribe, a gift of language, a good memory, and a sense of humor. They find a place for humor in their most solemn ceremonies like prayer, dancing, and worship.

"Humor is a serious thing," James Thurber once stated. "I like to think of it as one of our greatest resources, which must be preserved at all costs." A laugh can lighten most burdens and make us more human and open to God's grace. Preachers who can make people smile or laugh often make a difficult message more palatable or persuasive. One pastor was asking for money to plaster and paint the ceiling of the church. While he was making his appeal, a piece of plaster fell from the ceiling and hit a man on his head. The man jumped up and said, "Father, I will give $50!" After a pause, the pastor looked up to the ceiling and barked, "Lord, hit him again."

Good preachers realize humor sharpens our minds, gives a positive perspective on life, and above all, helps us to recognize the absurdities in life. Humor adds a twinkle to the gospels, and can spark a deeper appreciation of how Christ's spirit can touch people's lives in a deep and profound way.

We preachers need a holy humor that can touch even the grumpiest and cynical listener; we need a treasury of "ho-ho-holy" humor, a spirituality of laughter and joy. So we bow our heads and pray for just that.

13   THE PREACHER AS PROPHET

"With the help of the Holy Spirit, it is the task of the entire People of God, especially pastors and theologians, to hear, distinguish, and interpret the many voices of our age, and to judge them in the light of the divine Word." These words from the *Pastoral Constitution on the Church in the Modern World* present a challenge to any preacher, especially to the prophetic preacher.

This injunction was certainly the task of the prophets in Old Testament times. Through pointed parables and rich imagery they interpreted the events that were happening in the lives of the people, and tried to make them aware of God's will.

The two essential elements of a prophet are: hearing (and answering) a call from God, and the conviction to communicate a new vision. Walter Brueggemann describes the two jobs of a prophet as denouncing what is wrong, and announcing the vision of a just society. A prophet has to understand the present and be in touch with the past in order to create a just society. The prophet challenges listeners to understand that today is the sum accumulation of yesterday–as well the resource for tomorrow.

The prophet is a horizon-maker living in the experience of ultimates; he or she challenges a nation or people to live within a deeper religious experience. The primary work of the prophet is to proclaim reality. To do this, the prophet needs vision, which flows from God's inspiration. The prophetic community is then given a chance to respond to the message of the prophet or to reject it–as they often did.

Jesus was often rejected because of what he taught and preached.

He proclaimed a jubilee year in his famous synagogue speech (Lk 4:18–22). After saying this, he made some antagonistic statements that angered the people, and they led him to the top of a hill, ready to hurl him over (Lk 4:23–30). "But he passed through the midst of them and went on his way." Very few preachers will be able to escape unscathed, however, when challenging their listeners as Jesus did.

If we are to be prophetic preachers, we must be willing to acknowledge, as Stanley Hauerwas wrote, that:

> We are preaching to a Church in the midst of a war–a position you may find odd to be advocated by a pacifist....Who more than the Christian pacifist knows that Christians are in a war against war? I do not need something called the human condition illumined when I am preparing to face the enemy. Rather, I need to have a sense where the battle is, what the stakes are, and what the long-term strategy might be. But that is exactly what most preaching does not do. It does not help us locate our enemy, because it does not believe that Christians should have enemies.

Making a choice

The prophet realizes the word is powerful yet powerless; that is the ultimate paradox. A prophet preaches with the awareness of being a bridge over troubled waters.

The task of the prophet is to help change the reality of what is to the reality of what can be. To do this, we must first develop an awareness of where people are in their lives. Next, we must understand and grasp their experiences. Once we understand them, we can make a judgment about the nature of these experiences. Finally, we give people a choice. We help them to make a decision, always within the context of the love demonstrated over and over again by Jesus.

Prophetic preachers need to place Jesus at the center of reality, so listeners can make a choice about whether to respond to him or not. A positive choice demands a relationship to Jesus, who plays a central role in revealing God to us.

Scripture gives us many examples that involve a choice. When Jesus chose to be baptized by John in the Jordan river, he experienced an overwhelming sense of the Father's acceptance: "You are my Son, the Beloved; with you I am well pleased" (Mk 1:11). Jesus faced a threefold choice in the desert, when he was tempted by the devil (Mt 4:1–11). Throughout his ministry, Jesus made the choice to cherish the outcasts. Why was this so? As Albert Nolan, OP, points out in his book *Jesus Before Christianity,* it was because Jesus himself was an outcast.

Let's go back again to the story of Nathan confronting David about the death of Uriah (2 Sam 12:1–13). When he hears the story of the rich man taking the poor man's ewe, David becomes very upset, saying: "As the Lord lives, the man who has done this deserves to die...." All Nathan said in reply was: "You are the man!" Thus, God spoke to David through Nathan, and gave him a choice. David accepted the message and repented: "I have sinned against the Lord." Nathan answered, "Now the Lord has put away your sin: you shall not die."

This story could be used to point out an injustice that is being transacted in our society today. All of us (including the preacher) are often like David. We point a finger at others and fail to grasp that, though we might not be directly culpable for violence or crime, we are still responsible to a degree. Like David, we too are invited to repent.

Sensitive issues

How many of us are willing to preach about women in the church, homosexuality, assisted suicide, capital punishment, discrimination, AIDS, or the plight of the poor and hungry? We need to ask ourselves and our listeners questions like these: Are we guilty of taking women for granted? Do we listen to their pleas for equality? Have we read the document of the American bishops on gays and lesbians? Do we understand the "seamless garment" position of the Church in regard to the dignity of human life? Do we get close enough to the poor, hungry, marginalized, and homeless to allow these people to evangelize us?

Prophetic preachers need to disturb the complacent and comfort those in desperation, bringing new life, energy, and hope to our Christian world. A prophetic preacher must be extremely sensitive to injustices. Rabbi Abraham Joshua Heschel states: "To us a single act of injustice—cheating in business, the exploitation of the poor—is a slight; to the prophet, it is a disaster. To us, injustice is injurious to the welfare of the people; to the prophet, it is a deathblow to existence: to us, an episode; to them, a catastrophe, a threat to the world."

A prophet attempts to make people "feel fiercely" about what is going on in their world. Many people today are immune to violence, crime, ethnic cleansing, hunger, and poverty. As Walter Burghardt writes, "Now we can wolf down our pizzas and slurp our Schlitz to the roar of rockets and the flow of blood. It's commonplace; we see too much of it; it's part of the human tragedy. It no longer grabs our guts—no more than broken bodies in the Super Bowl."

Feeling fiercely cannot be faked, but arises from much prayer, hard work, and a deep compassion for the poor and marginalized. Prophets challenge us to new ways of thinking, provoke us to change our mindsets so we can see things differently. Those who strive to preach prophetically today must not be afraid to address issues that might rankle our listeners; for example, pointing out how individualism has gripped our country. (Sociologist Robert Bellah insists that the Church, of all the institutions, should counteract this peril, likened to a modern Baal.)

Are we willing to speak about the fact that workaholism can lead to spiritual bankruptcy, or that consumerism has a stranglehold on us and has turned the shopping mall into a cathedral? That car phones, video games, stereos, computers, and other electronic "toys" can become status symbols and signs of oppression? That most of us lead frenetic and frantic lives filled with too much stress and road rage, heading pell mell into a downward spiral? Prophetic preachers need to point out the idols in our society, like television, drugs, wealth, power, and a desire for material success.

To preach prophetically means that we will identify with Jeremiah, who felt he was duped: "For whenever I speak, I must cry out, I must shout, 'Violence and destruction!' For the word of the Lord has become for me a reproach and derision all day long" (Jer 20:8). Many of us would far prefer to hear people remark, "I enjoyed your sermon, Father," rather than have them walk out on us, or send us an acrimonious letter of protest. Yet as John Shea writes in *Gospel Light,* "Prophecy is not about pleasing people. It is about speaking the truth that no one wants to hear, the truth that is covered up by the comfortable." Prophetic preachers need to offer a vision, share insights, and open up new vistas so people can live the Christian life more fully.

Prophecy in the parables

The prophets of old were able to share the hopes and dreams of the people of Israel. They addressed human situations in concrete, down-to-earth language because they lived in solidarity with the people. In this same way, the parables give a strong message by using the language of the people of Jesus' day. Jesus took this language and shot it through with new meaning, with a new reality. He used ordinary examples like a farmer sowing his seed, a housewife looking for coins, vineyards, shepherds, banquets, and more.

The parable of the Good Samaritan asks the question: "Who is my neighbor?" The priest passed by the man because he did not want to be unclean by touching someone who might be dead. The Levite passed by because he was afraid he would be attacked when he tried to help the victim. Only the Samaritan—and herein lies the shock, because there was much animosity between Jews and Samaritans—would stop and help the wounded man.

In preaching on this parable, the prophetic preacher might ask the listeners which person do they identify with? What is their excuse for not stopping and helping the wounded man? How often do they see a motorist stranded on the highway and pass on by, not having the courage or compassion to stop and help? As one rabbi stated, "When you reach down to help others who have fallen in a ditch, you have to be prepared to get a little dirty yourself."

Another example is the parable of the laborers and the vineyard

(Mt 20:1–16). This story vividly portrayed the unemployment of Jesus' day. The laborers had been standing around idle because the rebuilding of the temple in Jerusalem had been completed, and work was scarce.

The situation was not unlike the corporate downsizing that went on in the 1980s, or the high unemployment seen in previous times. Receiving the heartrending news that after thirty years of working for a company, one's services are no longer needed can undoubtedly cause as much anger as that of the workers in the parable, who expected to be paid more because they had "borne the burden of the day and the scorching heat." (Concerning this parable, someone has remarked, "This is no way to run a railroad.")

Consider the possibility that those who worked for a shorter time accomplished just as much as those who labored all day. A skillful worker can accomplish more in a shorter span of time. Think of all the time consumed each day in some areas of the workplace where little work is done. What needs to be emphasized is that the workers agreed to the amount to be paid. Was it really envy that upset the workers? By their angry reaction, did they not judge those who labored less? These are some of the areas a prophetic preacher must point out to the assembly.

Another parable with the power to shock is that of the unjust steward (Lk 16:1–8). How could the master praise his dishonesty? Yet what should be highlighted is how wisely and prudently the steward acted in a crisis situation. The challenge of God's kingdom demands we too act prudently in times of crisis. Do we put God first in our lives? How do we relate to those in authority, especially when they are unjust? Are we faithful stewards of what has been entrusted to us? Some years ago, a factory in Massachusetts burned to the ground. Although none of the employees could work while the factory was being rebuilt, the employer continued to pay his employees. Many people considered this act of stewardship to be shocking.

We might compare this parable to the story about a couple who took their very small child to a movie. The usher reminded them, "If the baby cries, you'll have to leave, but we'll give you your money back." After watching the movie for a while, the husband asked the wife, "How do you like it? She whispered, "It's horrible." The husband agreed and said, "Pinch the baby."

Jesus showed courage in the face of rejection and vicious hatred. He embraced this evil and overcame it; he did not respond with hatred but with love because he knew he was beloved. This prompted him to say on the cross, "Father, forgive them; for they do not know what they are doing" (Lk 23:34).

We too need this kind of courage when we preach a message of nonviolence, advocate for a strong family life, encourage better education, or make people aware of rampant materialism. We need to proclaim how important it is to stand up for the dignity of all people, especially the oppressed, and encourage forgiveness instead of revenge.

Like Amos, Jeremiah, and Isaiah, prophets speak the truth regardless of the consequences. Jesus showed courage when he advocated nonviolent resistance: "if anyone strikes you on the right cheek, turn the other also" (Mt 5:39). He healed a woman, who had been bent over for eighteen years, on the Sabbath, angering the synagogue leader. He called the woman a daughter of Abraham in contrast to the Jews, who spoke only of the sons of Abraham.

Do we have the courage to speak the truth in love, as Paul preaches in Ephesians (4:15)? If we do, we must expect the same fate as the prophets who went before us. They threw Jeremiah into a cistern, and left him to die. Nelson Mandela was in a prison for over twenty years, and Martin Luther King, Jr., was jailed on a number of occasions before being assassinated. Joan of Arc was burned at the stake; her impact was felt only after her death.

And what happened to Jesus, the greatest prophet of all? They killed him. If this is what it means to preach prophetically, so be it! Volunteers, line up now.

14 BIBLICAL PREACHING

Recently, Catholic Theological Union professors Barbara Reid, OP, and Leslie Hoppe, OFM, organized a research project designed to show how preachers use Scripture in their homilies. They listened to over one hundred tapes of homilies given by over thirty priests ordained since 1970. In doing so, they found very few examples of effective preaching using Scripture.

The homilists who participated in the project felt that their seminary training had prepared them well for using Scripture. Reid and Hoppe concluded, however, that their inability to use Scripture well could be traced *precisely* to their seminary education. As a result of their findings, Reid and Hoppe invited professors of biblical studies and homiletics from seven different seminaries and schools of theology to a three-day consultation at the Catholic Theological Union in Chicago. The focus of the meeting was on the use of Scripture in preaching.

During the three days, the participants engaged in lively discussions on the nature of the homily. They profiled the student population in seminaries and theological schools today, examined the use of faculty resources, and reviewed efforts at continuing education. All agreed that more needed to be done to stress the need for biblical preaching.

The homily is an integral part of the liturgy, as pointed out in the *Constitution on the Sacred Liturgy:* "By means of the homily the mysteries of the faith and the guiding principles of the Christian life are expounded from the sacred text during the course of the liturgical year..." (#52). The document also insisted that "Preaching should draw its content mainly from scriptural and liturgical sources, being a proclamation of God's wonderful works in the history of salvation, the mystery of Christ…"(#35). Finally, *Fulfilled in Your Hearing* states: "The homily is not so much on Scripture as from and through them" (#50).

The *Constitution on Divine Revelation* (#25) urged preachers to delve into and study the Scriptures carefully. It is most important for preachers to listen inwardly to Scripture, because until we have internalized the texts, we have little or nothing to proclaim. Further, not only should we listen before preaching, but also listen as we preach. This is so we will not become "an empty preacher of the word of God outwardly, who is not a listener inwardly," as Pope John XXIII wrote in his encyclical *Pacem in Terris*.

It is also helpful to understand the difference between exegesis and hermeneutics. Hermeneutics is the science of interpreting scriptural texts, while exegesis is the practical application of that science, i.e., discovering the meaning and sense inherent in the text. Further, this interpretation of the texts strives to make Scripture relevant to people's lives today.

Good preaching, however, does not consist in strict explanation or interpretation of the texts. Preachers need to take over where the Bible leaves off. In *The Past, Present, and Future of Biblical Theology*, James Smart points out that, "The scholar has no access to the original meaning unless the text has some meaning for him now." Thus, preachers are challenged not so much to explain Scripture as to attempt to interpret our human situation through God's word.

In an article in the Fall 1998 issue of *Church*, Daniel Harrington describes the various tools of analysis needed to interpret a biblical text. He writes that a literary analysis consists in first paying attention to the context of the biblical text, then in examining the words and images contained in the text. In a historical analysis, the preacher is aware of how the text relates to its historical tradition, to ancient parallels, and to a concrete life setting. When these two steps have been completed, the preacher needs to reflect theologically on the text, then apply it to the present.

Donald Senior, CP, maintains that "a thorough working knowledge of the biblical text, a love of the biblical tradition, an instructive understanding of biblical history, a ready access to biblical symbols, a habitual use of the Bible in prayer, and an imaginative appreciation of the power of the Scriptures may do more to improve preaching than any other steps we might take."

A timeless message

The Bible is still the bestselling book in the world, far surpassing classics such as Plato's *Republic* or Homer's *Iliad*. Among all books in the Western world, the Bible stands alone. The Bible is thousands of years old and has no boundaries. No preacher will ever be able to exhaust its context and meaning, for here is portrayed human experience at its best and worst.

If the preacher has struggled with God's word and found a way to express the message forcefully, the preaching will not be characterized as lacking in content. Isaiah expressed it well: "So shall my word be that goes out from my mouth; it shall not return to me empty, but it shall accomplish that which I purpose, and succeed in the thing for which I sent it" (55:11). Or, as the book of Hebrews says, "Indeed, the word of God is living and active, sharper than any two-edged sword, piercing until it divides soul from spirit, joints from marrow; it is able to judge the thoughts and intentions of the heart" (4:12).

The Bible is a vast museum, and preachers are invited to roam through gallery after gallery, experiencing the ways in which God spoke to various peoples. Gregory the Great compared sacred Scripture to a vast river "where lambs wade and elephants swim." The Bible affirms as well as confronts. It can help people realize who they are, sons and daughters of a loving God. And so preachers must glean Scripture for the clues to God's presence in our lives, and the unpredictable depth of God's love. Our challenge is to recreate the faith dimensions found in the Bible, and convey this to our assemblies.

Biblical preaching does not mean we grant lip service to a few scriptural quotations, or that we pepper our homilies with scriptural references. It does mean that our preaching should be shaped by Scripture. The scriptural message should be the starting point as well as the foundation of our preaching. Biblical texts are not to be used to bolster or prove a doctrinal point or position.

God's words can cut to the very marrow of our listener's bones—as well as ours. And so, when we prepare our homily, we need to ask ourselves: is this based in God's word? Am I preaching the message that was meant to be conveyed in this passage, or am I using it to put across my own opinion? To answer those questions we need to ask ourselves another question: has God's word formed me, as well as shaped my preaching? Francis of Assisi, who loved Scripture, made a tongue of his whole body; the whole person spoke. In the same manner, we proclaim what we know and how we have been formed.

Augustine was known to improvise on biblical texts after much prayer and meditation. He was not known to be very orderly in his preaching, but he was fond of alliteration, antithesis, and assonance. Augustine encouraged participation from his audiences and delighted in applause. If we study his sermons, however, it becomes evident that they are biblical in character. For example, his explanation of the Sermon on the Mount "shows Augustine as a master of biblical preaching," according to Jaroslav Pelikan in *The Preaching of Augustine*.

Preaching purpose

A gospel passage that is often cited as an apt summary of the Bible's preaching purpose is this: "Therefore every scribe who has been trained for the kingdom of heaven is like the master of a household who brings out of his treasure what is new and what is old" (Mt 13:52). The scribe draws from the deepest core of oneself to enkindle a strong faith, and inspires others concerning God's presence in the world. The scribe also brings forth both the new and old, that is, creative, challenging, and refreshing ideas as well as traditional ones.

Jesus often referred to the Hebrew Scriptures as he proclaimed the good news and challenged his listeners. He resisted the devil in the desert by quoting Scripture three times (Mt 4:1–11). He used the famous passage from Isaiah (61:1), "The Spirit of the Lord is upon me..." to launch his public ministry. He quoted proverbs, spoke of the widows in the days of Elijah, gave only the sign of Jonah, and declared that "The stone that the builders rejected has become the chief cornerstone" (Ps 118:22).

Søren Kierkegaard once called Jesus "the contemporary eternal." The word of God is timeless, as well. The gospels often telescope people and events, not as occurrences of long ago, but as paradigms of the present. Preachers need to show how the faith experiences of their listeners are the same as those of Zacchaeus, Nicodemus, Peter, Martha, and Mary.

Paul called himself "a servant of Jesus Christ, called to be an apostle, set apart for the gospel of God" (Rom 1:1). It is evident from his writings how he was steeped in biblical language and history. Every good preacher needs to be the same, having a passionate love for the biblical texts and their meaning.

Scripture as seed

Jesus spoke of the power of the word as a seed. If we have ever held a seed in our hand, we know how tiny it is. Yet it holds more power in it than an atomic bomb. A seed found in an Egyptian tomb, estimated to be as old as two thousand years, sprouted when planted in soil. A seed is life-giving and produces far more than its original size.

But, as Barnabas Ahern, CP, wrote, "It is not sufficient to scatter God's word indiscriminately throughout a sermon as though it were an 'abracadabra' to light fire and to break the rock into pieces." A preacher needs to skillfully integrate God's word into the homily so that the message becomes compelling. A good preacher must choose the right seed and follow the rules for planting in order to reap a rich harvest. No farmer plants acorns if he wants a crop of corn. So too the preacher must use the precise words of Scripture to have a salutary effect on the audience.

Every farmer knows that well prepared soil is essential for seeds to grow; simply scattering the seed on any ground will not produce a good harvest (see Mark 4:3–9). Apt and precise quotations from the Scriptures will be effective only if the listeners are disposed to hear and understand them. Hence it is important for a preacher to use one's imagination and appeal to as many emotions as possible. Using good imagery also challenges our listeners. A comment such as, "Our

God is like fuller's earth," is obscure and won't provoke much of a response. But to liken our human trials to a "thorn in the flesh," as Paul speaks of, might produce a stimulating response.

Farmers also know that soil can be overworked, and so a rotation of crops is essential. Has our stock of Scripture passages become a bit threadbare because of overuse? The good preacher needs to search for alternate Scripture passages which might hold new meaning for the assembly. Expanding one's library of Scripture quotations and examples demands tireless work on the part of the preacher. There are no shortcuts in this process; it can only happen through reading, study, and prayerful reflection.

Above all, a preacher must live God's word. A planted seed needs to be nurtured with rain, sun, and all the other elements for it to grow. Preachers need to nurture their love for Scripture so it can penetrate their whole being and give them an urgency to proclaim the good news. Good preachers can change stone water jars into joyful wine, a wine that makes our listeners enthusiastic about the word of God. I doubt that any of us will ever be accused of being too much "filled with new wine," as the apostles were when the Holy Spirit descended on them (Acts 2:13).

By wrestling with the word of God, we will become much better preachers. By our fruits we will be known.

15 THE GOSPEL WELL PROCLAIMED

Remember the saying "The gospel well proclaimed is the homily half proclaimed"? A few medieval theologians even stated that the gospel reading was, in itself, a sermon. Eugene LaVerdiere, SSS, maintained, "Unless the word has been well read and actually heard, a good homily is all but impossible."

Randall Duk Kim is one of the founders of the American Players Theater in Spring Green, Wisconsin. He is noted for his performance of Shakespearean roles. At a clergy assembly some years ago, a priest asked Kim to give a Scripture reading. Taking the request seriously, Kim withdrew for ten minutes, then offered a stirring interpretation of the passage. During the discussion that followed, another priest asked Randall Duk Kim how he could play the same role night after night and not get bored. His answer? "I guess I just haven't gotten to the bottom of it yet."

Preachers need to ask the same question of themselves: How do we read or proclaim the gospel over and over again without it becoming boring? Truly, our answer to that question should be the same as that of Randall Duk Kim. Many priests and deacons read the gospel as if their voice is on automatic pilot. They give the impression that proclaiming the gospel is a burdensome job, something like reading a stock market report.

In her book *Oral Interpretation,* Charlotte Lee says this: "Oral interpretation is the art of interpreting a work of literary art in its intellectual, emotional, and aesthetic entirety." This definition can help us get to the bottom of a Scripture passage. We are challenged to interpret the richness of the gospel text and bring out its full meaning.

Mortimer Adler once defined a lecture as when "the notes of the professor become the notes of the student—without passing through the minds of either." Can people say the same about the way we read or proclaim the gospel, that it goes from the reader on to the hearer without passing through the mind of either?

To proclaim well, we first must imagine what we are about to do and say. If we visualize the circumstances in as fresh a manner as possible, it becomes easier to express the emotion contained therein. Then the challenge is to proclaim the gospel as if we were doing it for the first time. We need to imagine that we are Matthew, Mark, Luke, John—or Jesus. A good proclaimer tries to identify with the text and open oneself to its scriptural challenge.

What often distinguishes good proclamation from the ordinary is the ability of the speaker to fully understand the reading, and the desire to share this understanding with one's listeners. Few of us are able to read like Charlton Heston, Charles Laughton, Richard Burton, or Katharine Hepburn. But all of us can improve our reading skills so as to touch listeners in different ways or reveal hidden meanings in the text.

Another difference between poor and good proclamation can be found in how committed we are to the text. This commitment demands that we be attuned to the meaning of the words, the emotions, and the subtle shift of ideas and feelings. We can nourish our listeners with the richness we have discovered in the text. And so we ask ourselves, how can we best share the thoughts and feelings of the evangelists, or the words of Jesus?

The word of God

The new Code of Canon Law (1983) emphasized the connection between the gospel reading, which it calls "sacred text," and the homily. This is not some piece of literature, powerful as it might be, but God's inspired word. Thus, it must be proclaimed in that spirit.

The proclamation does not have to be done with a theatrical or rhetorical flourish, because proclaiming the gospel is not acting. We don't proclaim to perform but to communicate ideas. One who is good at proclaiming does so without imposing one's self on the assembly or by using a lot of theatrical fanfare. If we draw attention to ourselves rather than the text, we defeat the purpose of good proclamation.

After Mass one day, a certain parishioner was telling his pastor how much he appreciated the liturgy. Thinking it had something to do with his homily, the pastor asked him, "What was it that impressed you, Joe?" He responded, "The way you read the gospel. I never heard it read that way before."

Paul wrote to the Corinthians, "For I handed on to you as of first importance what I in turn had received..." (1 Cor 15:3). What is it that we hand on to our listeners when we proclaim God's word? A sense of reverence and awe for sacred Scripture? Or does the proclamation sound like Walker Percy's comment, "worn thin and long as used poker chips"?

Karl Rahner wrote about God's word as "primordial words," meaning first created or developed, earliest formed. He insisted that God's words "bring light to us, not we to them. They have power over us, because they are gifts of God, not human creations, even though perhaps they came to us through human beings." Talk about a reversal of roles!

In *The Spoken Christ*, Willard Jabusch writes this about irresponsible proclaimers:

> The nourishment that should come from the word of God is not received. A spiritual malnutrition sets in. An ennui and disdain for the Bible follows; the words of Scripture produce only a boring tastelessness. The whole liturgy begins to appear as a formality, heavy and unreal. Can it be saved by good preaching or fine singing? Perhaps. But the subtle message has been given that we need not really care about the word of God and its communication. It seems an unhappy waste of time, a burdensome job to be endured.

Preparation

A professor of homiletics at the Catholic University once stated, "If the clergy would prepare themselves for the reading of the gospel properly they would not have to preach on Sunday. To read the gospel well, with understanding and proper interpretation, takes much time and labor. A priest should keep in mind his sacred office of a lector and a messenger of the holy gospel."

How many of us who proclaim the gospel prepare well? Too often we look at the text and respond, "Oh, it's that one. I know it." If we have attended a concert, we know how the musicians tune up their instruments despite the fact that they are accomplished musicians. Likewise, we too need to prepare the gospel passage each time we are to proclaim it in order to become more attuned to its meaning. We should ask: What is the central idea? What is the most important part of the gospel? What will we emphasize or stress? Is there a climax? The deeper our understanding and impression of the text, the greater will be our expression in proclaiming it.

Often we prepare the gospel by reading it silently. Yet an oral reading can help in effective communication. It challenges us to be creative in our communication, especially by being more aware of correct phrasing. (A good rule to remember is that, all things being equal, the longer the phrase the better. Short phrases, especially when repeated, can add to choppiness in the delivery.)

We also need to sense the mood or feeling of the gospel text, especially when there is an obvious one. A good proclaimer has to imagine and recreate that feeling for the assembly. And so we don't just think about the ideas present in the text, but really feel them. For example, Peter and John rushed to the tomb to see if Jesus really rose from the dead; this passage demands a feeling of excitement. When Jesus is tempted three times in the desert, there is a feeling of finality when he says, "Away with you, Satan! for it is written, 'Worship the Lord your God, and serve only him'" (Mt 4:10).

Thought, imagination, and feeling are combined in good proclamation. Ideas without feeling or imagination remain cold. Feeling without thought produces sentimentality. Imagination without thought and feeling is simply not possible. All three elements blended together will insure an excellent proclamation of the gospel.

Manner of expression

The good proclaimer helps listeners to participate in the gospel message. In the time of Augustine, during the fourth century, people were known to applaud the reader. The liturgies in many African and Asian countries today can be very spirited gatherings, with dancing and singing and other demonstrative behavior. It is not necessary to have that type of response in our own churches, but the challenge remains for the proclaimer to help the assembly become engaged in God's word. As Bernard Lonergan stated, "The work of art is an invitation to participate."

A pause or silence is critical before and after important words or phrases in the gospel text. Once we have said, "A reading from the holy gospel according to Luke," we should pause even before we begin the gospel text. Yet many of us charge right on ahead and miss an opportunity for the listeners to become more attuned to what will follow.

In the Byzantine liturgy, the deacon exclaims, "Wisdom! Let us be attentive!" loud and clear, before the proclamation. We also need to pause at the end of the proclamation, before and after saying, "The gospel of the Lord." Many proclaimers have a tendency to move on rather than offer a moment of reflection. The assembly needs time to assimilate what has been proclaimed.

Imagine what might happen if we paused and looked intently at the congregation after reading these sacred words from the story of the prodigal son: "He refused to enter the house" (Lk 15:28), or after the words, "You are the salt of the earth....You are the light of the world" (Mt 5:13, 14). When we say the words of Thomas, "My Lord and my God!" how easy it is to move on immediately to what Jesus then said (Jn 20:28–29). We often rush through Jesus' words, "I am the way, and the truth, and the life," rather than pause after each phrase (Jn 14:6).

Another temptation is found when a question is asked within the text, for example, when Pilate asks Jesus, "What is truth?" Many proclaimers then speed ahead to the answer. We need to give listeners time to answer the question in their own minds. When an important statement is made, like the prodigal son saying, "I am no longer worthy to be called your son; treat me as one of your servants" (Lk

15:19), a pause or moment of silence can be far more forceful than the text itself.

Silence is God's language and can speak a powerful message. The mystic Meister Eckhart wrote, "There is nothing so much like God as silence." Yet many of us are uncomfortable with silence. Good proclamation always contains a certain amount of silence so God's word can be grasped more fully.

Many proclaimers keep their eyes glued to the text as they are reading it. Good eye contact helps to establish rapport with one's listeners, and can put them at ease. Some proclaimers keep bobbing their heads up and down, thinking that is what is meant by good eye contact. Some know the first part of a sentence well and have the rest of the text memorized so they can look at their listeners.

It can be difficult to determine just when to look up from the text. Also, proclaimers can lose their place in the text and thereby break the train of thought. A pause can help after a meaningful phrase or sentence. Once a thought or feeling is expressed it is good to maintain the eye contact.

What often helps eye contact is to take lectionary in your hands. You will probably find that it is much easier to maintain contact with your listeners while holding the book. This also enables the congregation to clearly see your entire face, and helps to convey the emotions expressed by means of our facial expression.

One of the best ways to establish and maintain good eye contact is by preparing the gospel well. Bishop Kenneth Untener of Saginaw has the gospel texts memorized, so he can proclaim them without looking at the lectionary. I know of a permanent deacon who does this as well, and he is most effective in proclaiming the gospel.

Recently, I heard a deacon proclaim the passage from John's gospel where Jesus appeared to the apostles after his resurrection. He boldly proclaimed Jesus' words to Thomas: "Put your finger here and see my hands. Reach out your hand and put it in my side. Do not doubt but believe" (20:26–29). The deacon showed his hand while saying this and also pointed to his breast. The expression on his face was one of invitation and compassion. It was a powerful experience for me and for the assembly.

Balance

Not every word in a phrase or sentence is of equal importance. A good proclaimer weighs the value of the thoughts and feelings that are contained in the text. Certain phrases carry the main idea, thought, or feeling, while others are subordinate to them, explanatory or descriptive. At times the repetition of a phrase can emphasize an important thought or feeling.

Key nouns and verbs are ordinarily emphasized. In some instances adjectives are important, but caution is needed in determining how necessary they are to the overall thought or feeling. If the wrong words are emphasized, it can distract from a meaningful communication of the gospel message.

Watch out for the last words of a sentence! Too many proclaimers have a tendency to trail off at the end of the sentence instead of emphasizing it. In many cases the last words build up to the climax of a particular gospel passage.

Some proclaimers read an entire gospel text at the same rate of speaking. Some parts of the gospel, like explanatory or descriptive passages that are not as important to the message, can be proclaimed at a faster rate. We must slow down at the important words, however. Too often, key phrases are tossed out too rapidly. I cannot imagine Jesus in the synagogue quickly saying: "TheSpiritoftheLordisuponmebecausehehasanointedmetobringgoodnewstothepoor..." (Lk 4:18). Proper variation of rate counteracts monotony, which is an enemy of good proclamation.

If it is true that the gospel well proclaimed is the homily half proclaimed, we can do much in this regard to contribute to the quality of our preaching. We need to get to the bottom of the gospel texts, and continue to explore the intellectual, emotional, and aesthetic aspects of the gospel. We must constantly remind ourselves that this is God's inspired word, sharper than any two-edged sword.

As preachers, we are charged with an important mission, that is, to break open God's word and make it relevant to the assembly. My hope is that this book has given you the incentive, along with practical ideas and suggestions, on how to better live out this mission in your ministry today.

RESOURCES

Ackerman, Diane. *A Slender Thread*. New York: Random House, 1997.

Atkinson, Brian. *How to Make Us Want Your Sermon*. New York: Joseph Wagner, 1942.

Bausch, William J. *A World of Stories for Preachers and Teachers*. Mystic, CT: Twenty-Third Publications, 1998.

Bausch, William J. *The Word: In & Out of Season*. Mystic, CT: Twenty-Third Publications, 2000.

Bernardin, Joseph. *The Gift of Peace*. Chicago: Loyola Press, 1997.

Bonham, Tal D. *The Treasury of Clean Church Jokes*. Nashville: Broadman Press, 1986.

Bonham, Tal D. *Humor: God's Gift*. Nashville: Broadman Press, 1991.

Boomershine, Thomas. *Story Journey: An Invitation to the Gospels of Storytelling*. Nashville: Abingdon Press, 1988.

Brueggemann, Walter. *Texts Under Negotiation*. Minneapolis: Fortress Press, 1993.

Brueggemann, Walter. *The Bible Makes Sense*. Winona, MN: Saint Mary's Press, 1997.

Burghardt, Walter, SJ. *Preaching: The Art and the Craft*. Mahwah, NJ: Paulist Press, 1987.

Burghardt, Walter, SJ. *Preaching the Just Word*. New Haven: Yale University Press, 1996.

Burke, John, editor. *A New Look at Preaching*. Collegeville, MN: Liturgical Press/ Michael Glazier, 1983.

Castle, Anthony. *A Treasury of Quips, Quotes, and Anecdotes for Preachers and Teachers*. Mystic, CT: Twenty-Third Publications, 1998.

Cone, James H. *God of the Oppressed*. Maryknoll, NY: Orbis Books, 1997.

Craddock, Fred. *Preaching*. Nashville: Abingdon Press, 1985.

Donders, Joseph. *With Hearts on Fire: Reflections on the Weekday Readings of the Liturgical Year*. Mystic, CT: Twenty-Third Publications, 1999.

Ford, Kevin Graham. *Jesus for a New Generation*. Downers Grove, IL: Intervarsity Press, 1995.

Freidl, Francis P. and Ed Macauley. *Homilies Alive: Creating Homilies that Hit Home.* Mystic, CT: Twenty-Third Publications, 1993.

Fulfilled in Your Hearing: The Homily in the Sunday Assembly. Washington, DC: United States Catholic Conference, 1982.

Fuller, Gerard, OMI. *Stories for All Seasons: For Every Sunday, Every Year.* Mystic, CT: Twenty-Third Publications, 1996.

Hardiman, Russell, editor. *At the Heart of Liturgy: An Essential Guide for Celebrating the Paschal Mystery.* Mystic, CT: Twenty-Third Publications, 1999.

Jabusch, Willard. *The Spoken Christ.* New York: Crossroad Publishing Co., 1990.

Jensen, Richard. *Thinking in Story.* Lima, OH: CSS Publishing Co., 1993.

Keating, Thomas, OSB. *Intimacy with God.* New York: Crossroad Publishing Co., 1994.

Lee, Charlotte. *Oral Interpretation.* Boston: Houghton Mifflin, 1982.

Manton, Joseph, CSSR. *Ten Responsible Minutes: A Pleasant Approach to Homily Headaches.* Huntington, IN: Our Sunday Visitor, 1978.

McKenna, Megan. *Not Counting Women and Children: Neglected Stories from the Bible.* Maryknoll, NY: Orbis Books, 1994.

Meyers, Robin. *With Ears to Hear: Preaching as Self-Persuasion.* Cleveland, OH: Pilgrim Press, 1993.

Mitchell, Henry. *Celebration and Experience in Preaching.* Nashville: Abingdon Press, 1990.

Nolan, Albert, OP. *Jesus Before Christianity.* Maryknoll, NY: Orbis Books, 1976.

Pelikan, Jaroslav. *The Preaching of Augustine: Our Lord's Sermon on the Mount.* Minneapolis: Fortress Press, 1973.

Schwarz, Anthony. *Media: The Second God.* New York: Random House, 1981.

Shea, John. *Gospel Light.* New York: Crossroad Publishing Co., 1998.

Smart, James. *The Past, Present, and Future of Biblical Theology.* Louisville: Westminster/ John Knox Press, 1979.

Tonne, Arthur. *Jokes Priests Can Tell.* Hillsboro, KS: Multi-Business Press, 1983.

Wogaman, Philip J. *Speaking the Truth in Love: Prophetic Preaching to a Broken World.* Louisville: Westminster/ John Knox Press, 1998.

Untener, Kenneth. *Preaching Better.* Mahwah, NJ: Paulist Press, 1999.

Of Related Interest...

This Sunday's Scripture Homily Service

This Sunday's Scripture truly is a "preacher's dream team," featuring talented authors Paul Holmes, Alice Camille, Michael Kent, and Bill Bausch. They offer you the material for a process of pondering the Word, of feeling it, tasting it, praying it, making it your own, to then communicate it more effectively to the people of your faith community. Fr. Paul Boudreau is the author of *The Weekday Readings*, the weekday supplement to *This Sunday's Scripture*. His reflections can serve as the basis for weekday homilies, or as a springboard for personal reflection.

Single subscription, one year: Mail: (monthly packet) $69.00 per year (Canada: $79.00 U.S.; outside of No. America, add $5.00). E-mail: (sent weekly, 11 days prior) $59.00 per year.

The Word: In and Out of Season
Homilies for Preachers, Reflections for Seekers
William J. Bausch

These sixty homilies—divided according to liturgical seasons, feasts, and celebrations, with a section on parables and lessons from Scripture—are presented to preachers as aids, thought-starters, or outright models. Witty, touching, full of humanity and wisdom, *The Word: In and Out of Season* belongs on the bookshelf and in the hands of every preacher, teacher, and seeker.   ISBN: 1-58595-003-3, 304 pages, $14.95

With Hearts on Fire
Reflections on the Weekday Readings of the Liturgical Year
Rev. Joseph Donders

This is an inspiring series of reflections on Jesus and his proclamation of the reign of God. It looks at Christ's vision of that reign and what we can do to bring his vision to reality in our lives and in our world. A wonderful companion for celebrating and reflecting on the weekday liturgy.   ISBN: 0-89622-974-2, 352 pp, $19.95

Scripture in Church (CD-Rom)
Commentaries and Homily Guidelines for the 3-year Lectionary Cycle
From *Doctrine and Life*, a Dominican publication (Ireland)

Scripture in Church offers you: an easy-to-use search and view system that will search through over 20,000 texts by occasion and year, verse reference, authors, theme or subject; up to 8 commentaries for each day by world-renowned homiletic and Scripture scholars; a variety of homiletic notes, celebrant's guides, and more; 3 translation options: NAB, NRSV, JB. Windows Requirements: DOS 6.0 or higher; Windows 3.1 or higher; 386 or higher; 8 MB RAM.   A-71, $129.00

Available at religious bookstores or from:

TWENTY-THIRD PUBLICATIONS

PO BOX 180 • 185 WILLOW STREET 🔲 MYSTIC, CT 06355 • 1-800-321-0411
FAX: 1-800-572-0788 BAYARD E-MAIL: ttpubs@aol.com

Call for a free catalog